Kangaroos
in Austria

Diane DeArmond

ISBN: 978-1-54395-153-0

Contents

FORWARD

Four years ago, at age fifty, I found myself divorced, broke, and living in one of the most expensive cities in the world: Newport Beach, California.

I had been married for twenty-four years to the father of my two children when I asked for a divorce. The marriage had long been an unhappy one. I moved out of our home in the vineyards of Temecula, California and into a small apartment in Newport Beach. I had lived in Newport before my parents moved us inland when I was thirteen years old. My father thought Newport Beach was a materialistic community with shallow values, but later, as an adult, I must admit that I was attracted to the idea of moving back to the affluent city of my early childhood.

After the divorce, my son Kevin went off to college in Northern California and my daughter Christina moved in with me temporarily. She was attending the local university and dating her high school sweetheart. Things were going pretty well for both of my children.

After a few short job stints, I ended up working at a boutique on Balboa Island in Newport Beach. My income was barely enough to cover my monthly expenses, and the divorce left me without any alimony. I was living day-to-day, hoping everything would work out.

Then, in a period of one month, Christina lost both her job and her boyfriend. Frustrated with life, she wanted to get away from it all and booked a ten-day trip to visit a friend of hers who had moved to Germany. Two days before her flight, her friend canceled the visit, and Christina was left with a round-trip ticket to Germany but no place to stay. She remembered that a professor of hers had moved to Graz, Austria. She contacted him, and he said that if she took a train from Germany to Austria, they could meet up at one of the city's many affordable hotels, and he would be her tour guide. It sounded great, so that's how Christina ended up in Austria instead of Germany.

A few months after Christina's return to Newport, we discussed our mutual longing for a simpler life and a way out of the rat race that dominated Newport culture. Christina proposed, "Why don't we sell everything we own and move to Europe?" I thought about it, and realized that there really wasn't any reason to stay in Newport. After all, I had found the dating scene in this beach town less than ideal. I'll spare you the details, but let's just say that my interactions with a few gentleman callers convinced me that my father might have had a point about the place.

Besides, I had lived in Southern California my entire life, and the thought of living somewhere completely different intrigued me. I did my homework on the options for living abroad, but what mattered most to me was that wherever we ended up needed to be safe and affordable. I wanted a pedestrian-friendly city so we wouldn't need a car. Good weather, nice people, and unique architecture would be great as well. Christina's Graz met all of those requirements. German was the language spoken in Graz, and I concluded that I would pick it up best just by living there.

So it was decided. However, just five months before we were supposed to move, Christina was accepted into veterinary school in Dublin,

Ireland. "What do we do now?" Christina asked. I told her, "You go to Ireland. I will go to Austria."

I received mixed reviews when I told friends and family about my decision. My family thought living abroad would be good for me, and they were very supportive, saying, "If anyone can do it, it's you!" But mostly, people thought it was just short of crazy to pick up and go to a place so far from home, in a part of the world I had never been.

Which brings me to the title of this memoir. When I brought up Austria in casual conversations, people would ask "Australia?" and I would say "No, Austria." I heard that a lot, actually. I didn't know why that was, but when I finally got to Austria, I found out: I saw key chains and souvenirs that stated, THERE ARE NO KANGAROOS IN AUSTRIA. Apparently, it's a common and rather silly misunderstanding, but it stuck with me and I developed a certain attachment to it. As an American in Graz, there were times when I felt (and probably seemed to others) like a misfit -- a kangaroo in Austria.

I spent the few remaining months before my departure selling everything I had. My Mercedes was paid for and I had some nice furniture. In the end I had enough money to at least start a new life. Finally, on March 4, 2011, I got on a plane with five 50-lb. suitcases and headed to Austria.

As for the current enterprise -- the account you're now reading -- I never set out to write a book. I just wanted to keep my family and friends updated on my progress, so I wrote emails when the spirit moved me and I thought the news was worth relating. As it turned out, those emails were passed around pretty broadly, and people I had never met started asking the senders for more. Friends suggested that I turn the adventures I had enjoyed sharing with them into a book. What follows is the result. I hope they give you as much pleasure in reading as I found in living them. Here goes!

ARRIVING IN GRAZ

It was a cold winter morning when I arrived in Graz. The trees were bare, and it was raining just enough to get my suitcases wet. I had booked a hotel located within walking distance of the center of the city. I made a two-week reservation hoping that in that time I could find a place to live. I found Hotel Mariahilf online and it looked quaint and friendly. It was located near the Mur and the Kunsthaus, a landmark museum. When I walked into my hotel the manager, Dominik, a twenty-five-year-old Austrian, greeted me. You should have seen his face when I walked through the door with my pile of luggage. He struggled with what to say and was amazed that I had traveled with so much stuff. He had blond hair and blue eyes that twinkled when he smiled.

We worked together to shove everything into the tiny elevator and send me to my room. The hotel was charming. My room was on the top floor with two small dormer windows that were set too high to see out of. I stood on the bed to look outside. I loved the many red rooftops that were sprinkled about. I had two beds, so I used one as extra storage for my things and quickly got everything squared away. I looked around downstairs and found a quaint dining room that served breakfast every morning. The lobby was small and had a steady flow of travelers.

The first night was great! I went to the pub directly across the street, and when I opened the door, the thick cigarette smoke that came barreling out blew me away. I walked back outside and went to the restaurant next door. This one had less smoke and three elderly men playing live music. The place was really rustic, with wooden picnic tables and wood floors. There were black-and-white photos and other memorabilia mounted on the walls. There was an old woman wearing an apron who greeted me with a menu. She didn't speak any English, and the menu was in German. I looked around the room and saw someone eating a grilled cheese sandwich at a nearby table. When the waitress returned, I pointed to the sandwich, and she understood. When the singing trio learned that I was from California, they burst into a rendition of "You Are My Sunshine." Before I knew it, the whole place was singing to me and I just clapped and smiled. My father used to sing that song to me when I was little, so I was pleasantly surprised to hear it in Austria. I had come all this way to find something new, only to be reminded of my childhood. I found that comforting.

The next morning at breakfast, I met a forty-five-year-old woman named Mitra. We quickly realized that we both spoke English, so we decided to share a table. She said that it was her first time in Austria and she was there to teach yoga classes for a few weeks. She had big brown eyes, dark skin, and long dreadlocks. There was something intriguing about her. In her eyes I saw a spiritual woman comfortable in her own skin. She had a peaceful way of talking that made me feel I could trust her. We talked for a while and made plans to meet in the lobby at 6:30 p.m. to go out for dinner.

At 6:30, I met Mitra and another hotel guest named Christine. Mitra had met the twenty-three-year-old earlier, and she was visiting from Germany. The three of us grabbed our coats and headed out to find someplace fun to eat. The sun was beginning to set and the city lights were calling.

I hadn't journeyed far from the hotel at this point. I was learning the area nearby and found a small market, a few cafes and shops. Nothing looked particularly exciting or noteworthy. This night with my new friends I walked across a bridge and into the center of the city called Hauptplatz. Hauptplatz was a beautiful square with large Gothic buildings and Renaissance courtyards. The buildings were painted in many different colors and were all lit up like Disneyland. We marveled at the beauty before us. I didn't realize that all of this was just over the bridge; I was ecstatic to see it unfold before me. Mitra was swept up in the moment, and with her arms open wide she spun around the cobblestone streets like a little girl. Christine and I found her excitement contagious and the three of us skipped down the street laughing. As I look back on this first experience now, I realize that even though we were three very different people, we were sharing the same intimate delight.

We decided on Stern, a quaint restaurant surrounded by shops and cafés. We were seated in a back room that was lit by the many candles that were placed on tables, windowsills, and ledges. Christine talked about her life in Germany. She was a student studying abroad in Graz. She was very shy and reserved, and I got the feeling that her family upbringing was strict. She chose her words very carefully. Mitra talked about life in India, and seemed to have a polar-opposite personality compared to Christine. Mitra spoke as though we were sitting around a campfire while she amused us with her stories. She described a time when her family didn't have any money and she was married off at an early age. I couldn't imagine what that would be like or living in India for that matter. I talked about my dream to make a new life for myself in Graz. I shared with them my hopes of obtaining a visa and a job. We were so engrossed in our conversation that the rest of the world didn't exist. There was just our passion for life and focused interest on each other. It was such a lovely night as we wondered back to the hotel, talking and laughing.

The next night I ventured out on my own to a small restaurant around the corner. There I had a glass of wine with a large plate of pasta. As I looked out the window, I saw a full moon beside an incredible clock tower. I saw streetlights flicker as the sweet people of Graz rode by on their bicycles and couples walked their dogs, hand in hand. Inside, the music playing was *The Phantom of the Opera's,* "Music of the Night." I was enchanted and hoped never to leave this poem.

DOMINIK

I knew I couldn't live in a hotel for too long, so I needed to find a place to rent. Dominik recommended his realtor friend Gerard. Gerard agreed to meet with me the next day and show me some flats in my price range. I liked him right away. I guessed him to be in his late thirties and he had a cheerful disposition. I thought it was nice of him to help me free of charge. He spoke English and we discussed what I was looking for. I wanted something close to Hauptplatz. There I would be near everything the city had to offer. Banking, grocery stores, the opera house, restaurants, everything I wanted would be in walking distance and the tram passed through every ten minutes. He spent the day showing me different flats, and by the end of that day, I had found the perfect one for me. The building was constructed in the early eighteen hundreds. From the sidewalk, we walked through the stone-and-brick lobby of one building, through a garden, and into my building. A quick climb up the concrete steps, turn left, and there was my flat.

It was small, but charming. The ceilings were twelve feet high and the windows were unlike any I had ever seen before. The first set were mounted on the outside of the building and the other on the inside, creating a window inside a window. The doorjambs were two feet thick, and all the floors were wood. The owner had remodeled the inside with all new kitchen appliances and fresh paint. The lighting in each room was a light bulb hanging from a wire. I needed drapes, rugs, a bathroom mirror, a closet, a bed, a couch, etc. I couldn't wait to move in!

I stayed in the hotel for an additional two weeks while waiting to finalize the lease on my flat. Dominik had been kind enough to offer me the hotel's best suite free of charge until my flat was ready. The suite belonged to the *Honorarkonsulat der Republik Kasachstan.* Apparently, he wasn't in Austria very often, and I got to have it all to myself.

One night after I had been out sightseeing, I ran into Dominik in the hotel lobby. It was around midnight, and the lobby was empty. He stopped me before I made it to the elevator, and he had a bottle of champagne and two glasses in his hand. "Would you like to join me? I need to sample this champagne to see if I want to serve it in my hotel!" This sounded a little suspicious, but I had no reason to doubt the man's intentions, so I thought, "Why not?"

We sat down in the comfortable seating area near the fireplace, and he opened the champagne. He was really cute, but he was also only twenty-five years old. He flirted with me while we drank champagne, and I have to say I was enjoying the company. Then, suddenly, he looked me straight in the eye and asked me to have sex with him. Just like that! I told him as nicely as I could that although he was very sweet, I only dated older men. He seemed surprised by my answer, but I kept insisting, and when I stood up to leave I leaned in and gave him a quick kiss on the cheek. This seemed to appease him, and off I went to my *Honorarkonsulat* suite. What struck me about Dominik's proposal was how matter of fact or simplistic it was. It was no big deal for him to suggest sex. His delivery sounded like it was just the way Europeans, or at least Austrians, conducted them selves. I also remember his face. His expression suggested that he expected me to say yes. I felt that this attitude might be something I would be dealing with in my new world.

MITRA

Mitra and I continued to meet every morning at breakfast. Whenever possible, we would meet later somewhere for dinner. I loved listening to her talk about her daily experiences in Graz. She told me that she had never really wanted to visit Austria. I asked her "why not Austria?" She then told me that she couldn't understand how the Austrian people could stand by and allow Hitler to destroy so many lives.

Broad assumptions like that, it seems, have a way of being tested. Later that day, an Austrian woman involved with the yoga studio where Mitra was teaching invited her to a private dinner party. She attended, and when that night passed I saw Mitra at our usual breakfast table. I grabbed my coffee and joined her. She looked different. Her face had softened and betrayed a hint of sadness. "What happened at your dinner?" I asked.

She told me that it was at a very large home with an elderly woman as the hostess. There were approximately ten people in attendance and Mitra was the guest of honor. The food and conversation were interesting, and coffee was served towards the end. As the hostess stood to clear the table, Mitra asked her this question: "How could your people stand by and let Hitler devastate your country?"

The elderly woman quietly sat down and answered. "I was a very young girl when the Germans invaded. I remember one day in particular when I was standing on our balcony. I saw three German soldiers in the distance and they were forcing a neighbor down to the ground. I ran inside, grabbed a couple of oranges, and threw them as hard as I could at the soldiers. When I returned home from school that day, my house was empty. The Germans had imprisoned my family, and I never saw them again." Mitra looked at her with tears in her eyes and apologized.

We sat quietly, finishing our coffee, realizing how little we knew about Austria and how much there was to learn, how painful the process of learning itself can be. There are the large, sometimes terrible facts you can find in history books, and then are the intimate, lived histories of the individuals who acted and suffered in perilous times. Both need attention if we want to come close to knowing what it was like to go through something like World War II.

After the big dinner, Mitra had two weeks left of her yoga seminars. One day, she insisted that I attend one of her classes. She traveled the world teaching yoga, and was considered to be quite the expert. I had never taken a yoga class, and frankly, I was never interested. I didn't know what to wear that day, but Mitra reassured me that a tank top and comfortable pants would be fine.

Well, I showed up at the yoga studio and instantly felt like a fish out of water. Everyone there was wearing leotards and running around barefoot. Mitra greeted me with a smile, but before we could talk, people wanting her attention surrounded her. "Can I get you a glass of water, Mitra?" "Do you need any tea?" "Is the temperature of the room okay?" It was like she was a celebrity. I was surprised to see people treating her with such reverence. I had seen her name on posters and newspapers in Graz, but had never given it much thought.

There were approximately twenty-five people in the class that night. Mitra stood at the front of the room with an interpreter by her side. She spoke in English, and her instructions were translated into German.

We warmed up with some stretching and then moved on to yoga positions. I was completely awkward and almost fell down. I couldn't get my body to extend or find any balance. Everyone else was doing yoga positions with ease. After about forty minutes, we were instructed to lie down on our backs with our eyes closed. We took some deep breaths and, through the filter of translation, were instructed to relax. The lights were dimmed, and Mitra lit a small candle. She then rang a tiny bell and began to issue a hum that soon turned into a monotone singing. I could feel myself begin to relax, and I felt her voice travel through my body. Suddenly, in my mind, I found myself soaring over fields that were glowing with golden light. Next, I was racing over the ocean and then above a desert. These feelings and images were quite unexpected, and I really couldn't explain them, didn't know what to make of them.

The lights came back on and we all stood. I wondered if anyone else had had that same experience. Later, I told Mitra about it, and she said that what I had experienced was something many people in yoga reach for and only a few ever achieve. I am thankful that I hadn't heard about it before that night, because my mind would have gotten in the way and it never would have happened. But then, that's how I'm told yoga works: ultimately, the idea is just to "let things happen" rather than making them happen. You can't force a feeling of freedom. I had gained some insight into myself that evening, and it was good to be reminded that not every piece of insight comes as painfully as the one Mitra found in questioning that old Austrian woman.

There's painful and then there's just plain awkward, and the latter is the theme for my next experience in Graz. A few days after the yoga class I attended, Mitra asked me if I had been to the Wellness Center. I told her that I had not, and she said it was a relaxing place with many saunas and pools. "You'll love it!" she said.

We took the tram towards the mountains and got off at the entrance to a large building. We paid a small fee to enter and headed for the dressing rooms. Right away, I noticed that everything was coed. In the locker room, Mitra and everyone around us started taking off their clothes and putting them into the lockers. I looked over at Mitra, and she was naked. She told me to hurry up so we could get into the water.

I didn't want to make a big deal about it, so I took off my clothes and quickly wrapped a towel around myself. Little did Mitra know that I was uncomfortable wearing a bathing suit in public, let alone being naked.

I didn't grow up in a naked house. Meaning that some households are comfortable in the privacy of their own homes to be seen naked by family members. This was not the case in my household. I remember walking into my mother's closet one day and she was half dressed. I could feel the awkwardness as she rushed to cover up. While in high school gym class, shower time was horrifying for me. I managed to get through four years of locker time with out ever taking a shower. Even in my twenty-four year marriage I never walked around the house naked. The insecurity of not looking good enough always haunted me.

Wrapped in the protection of my towel, we walked down a hallway that opened up to a very large room filled with pools, waterfalls, saunas, and Jacuzzis, just like Mitra had described. The very high ceiling was a glass atrium. Men and women of all ages were walking around naked -- swimming naked, reading the newspaper naked, eating a burger naked. Not a stitch of clothing on any of them! My head was spinning. My thoughts raced from oh my God how did I end up here; to how could these people be comfortable being so exposed. They were so nonchalant as if it didn't matter how anyone looked or if anyone was looking.

Mitra left me to go sit in a sauna, and I stood there trying to find an escape route. I saw a bubble filled Jacuzzi to my left and slowly edged my way in that direction. There were two people settled in and I was going to try to be the third. I averted my eyes hoping that if I didn't look at them they wouldn't look at me. I was hiding beneath the bubbles and gradually started to take a look around. The woman closest to me was in her sixties, overweight, and sagging breasts. Her head was tilted back and her eyes were closed as she blissfully soaked in the warm water. I on the other hand was in the fetal position with my arms wrapped around my tucked in legs. It occurred to me that if I saw anyone I knew I would be devastated. What if I ran into Gerard, my cute young realtor? "Oh hey, Gerard! How you doin'?" I would *die!*

After about forty-five minutes of not moving, I started to settle down. "This isn't so bad," I thought to myself. "See how relaxed everyone looks?" There was a large regular swimming pool approximately ten steps away. I really wanted to get over myself and make it to the other pool. This would mean that I would have to stand up and walk naked in front of everyone. I was completely aware that no one cared about my presence but it was still a lot for me to process. I gathered up enough courage to get out of the Jacuzzi. With each step my mind exploded. Am I walking too fast? Do I have bad posture? Am I standing out like a sore thumb? I made it to the pool and soon I was up to my neck in water. I saw a mysterious cave that had red lights in it, and I decided to investigate. It wasn't very large, just an empty cave with some built in seating. When I swam out, there were two men in their late thirties just sitting on the side of the pool with their feet in the water. I swam by, pretending it was something I did every day, and hoped they didn't notice me.

Eventually, Mitra showed up at my pool, and I asked her if she was ready to go. We had been there for two hours. How much time can you spend in the water, anyway? We went back to the dressing room, and I was proud of myself for trying something new. Just when I was thinking that this really was such an innocent, natural way to live, a man in his late forties came up to me as I was putting on my last piece of clothing. He put his hand on my back and said, "Hey, where have you been? I didn't see you in here! Want to go have a drink?" "Slimeball!" I thought.

Mitra and I left and went back to the hotel for the night. I am glad I tried the "naked sauna," but it wasn't something this modest American would do again. Maybe that's a good thing or maybe it's a bad thing, but that's the way it is.

IT TAKES A VILLAGE

I had been in Graz for three weeks, and my flat was going to be ready for me to move in the following week. I wanted to visit my daughter Christina in Ireland, and my son Kevin was going to be there for a few days, so I researched flights online. I had never traveled with Ryanair before, but they had incredibly low rates, so I gave the company a shot. I found that I was not able to book connecting flights together, but instead had to book each flight separately. When I booked my flight from Graz to Ireland, the only route was to fly to London, and then from London to Ireland. I won't bore you with the details, but it took me about three hours to figure out the three airports in London and the different arrival and departure times and get them all to match up.

First, I flew from Graz to London. While on the plane, I showed my connecting flight information to the flight attendants, and they all agreed that I was not going to make it. I was sitting in the very front of the plane, so the conversation between myself, the four flight attendants, and the surrounding passengers was a little like what you might hear in a coffee lounge.

Everyone got involved, as my plight became the topic of the moment. "You will never make your connecting flight, because you need at least an hour and a half and you have less than an hour." This was the consensus of the passengers.

"You also have to take into consideration that the security lines are longer on this day of the week, and because you don't have an EU passport, you have an additional line to wait in." This was the wisdom of the flight attendants. Then, a dashing young pilot in uniform spoke up from the seat behind me: "If you would like, I can escort you, and I might be able to cut some corners." I told him that I would be running, and I would understand if he wasn't up for a jog. He said, "No problem, I could use the exercise!"

When the plane landed, off we went! We ran through the airport, and at every long line that I was required to wait in, the pilot ran to the front and explained my situation. The sea of passengers literally parted as I ran through each section. When we reached the passport control window, there were a lot of people waiting, and the pilot was having a difficult time with the officials. It was taking too long, when I noticed the gentleman who had been seated next to me on the plane waving to me from up ahead. "I told them all about you, and they said come on through!" He yelled rather proudly. I was a bit overwhelmed. It's not like I'm transporting a human heart, I thought, but what the hell! I ran through the line and he let me go in front of him. After that line, I took off running again.

Eventually, the pilot caught up to me and we kept on running. We made it to the gate just in time. The pilot and I were standing side by side, sweating and panting, when I asked him if he had some other reason to be at that terminal. He said, "No, actually I'm off work and I live in London. I just wanted you to make your flight." How nice was that? I thanked him profusely, and we exchanged email addresses. With all the travel nightmares we hear about these days, here was an experience that came complete with a knight in shining armor, a dramatic series of sprints to the boarding area, and, finally, success.

SWEET IRELAND

My trip to Ireland was delightful. I got to spend time with both of my kids in Dublin, a place that was quaint and welcoming. I hadn't seen Kevin since moving to Austria and he hadn't been to Ireland before. Christina was looking forward to sharing her new life with us. After returning to Graz, I reflected on the wonderful time we had together.

One night in particular stood out as special. Kevin and I joined Christina and a couple of her friends for an evening of food, drink, and Irish folklore. It really was charming. The setting was the oldest pub in the entire country. We were seated at communal tables of eight or more and got to know the people at our table over some great local fare. Then, our host stood in front of a fireplace and talked about the history of Ireland and their belief in fairies. The fairies, it seems, were a magical people from long ago who retired to live in the underworld. They would come out at certain times to trick, imprison, or even kill unwary people. So it was never sensible to cut down a fairy tree (hawthorn, elder, or blackthorn), or move certain stones. One must also protect the house and any animals from the fairies, usually by putting iron on the doors and windows or planting special trees such as the rowan. Even today there are still "fairy trees" that farmers refuse to remove from their property, just in case.

When we were finished, we walked to a pub that had sparkling white lights all around and three musicians playing fun Irish music. We ordered our drinks and sat down. The place was tiny, but stuffed full with people. I liked that the lighting had very warm gold tones and was dim like candlelight -- it suited the packed intimacy of the place much better than the glare of bright lights.

After a few minutes, the band stopped to take a break. Suddenly, a man in his seventies stood in front of the band and called for our attention as he recited a poem he had written. I don't remember his exact words now, but he stood before us talking about history, brotherhood, and the need to stand together to fix our broken world. It moved me, and I noticed a tear run down my cheek. I really didn't want anyone to see, so I turned my head away from our group and only Christina noticed, silently. Here we were in a time of conflicts with other countries and natural disasters like the huge earthquake and tsunami Japan had suffered not long ago, destroying thousands of lives; a time of shooting rampages in America and political unrest in so many other lands. The simplicity of this man speaking from his heart (in a land that has known, after all, more than its share of sorrow and suffering) was touching and beautiful.

MOOSE JAMMIES

Back in Graz, my flat was finally ready for me. It was time for me to move out of the hotel. Gerard was scheduled to pick me up at the hotel, take me to sign the final contracts, and give me the keys. I got up a little early and started looking through my luggage for something to wear. I had just returned from Ireland the night before, and my things were spread out all over the place.

In the suite was a front door that led to a kitchen. To the left of that was the door to a large bathroom, and straight ahead was the door to the bedroom, a large meeting room, and the living room. I finished my shower and was going back and forth from the bathroom to the bedroom, grabbing toiletries. I was afraid that in my rush to get ready I might misplace the room key, so I left it in the bedroom door. I was in the bathroom when I realized that I needed my hairdryer. I tried to go back in to get it and *the door was locked!* "Noooooooooo! This can't happen!" There I was with a towel on my head, purple jammie pants, bare feet, and a gray jammie top that had a cartoon moose on the front. Now, if the moose wasn't bad enough, he was wearing a separate piece of fabric sewn onto his neck to look like a purple plaid scarf! I sat down on the floor and couldn't stop saying, "No! No! No!"

The last thing I wanted on my last day in the hotel was to be seen like this. I couldn't get to my clothes, curling iron, shoes, lipstick, anything. I had to go down to the hotel lobby with a towel on my head, barefoot and in moose jammies. As I walked down the stairs towards the front desk, I kept my head down. I approached the receptionist's desk and explained my predicament. She then informed me that because foreign diplomats stay in that suite, it had a special bulletproof door to the bedroom. There wasn't a second key. I had locked the only key on the inside of my room. The receptionist also said that Dominik was going to take me to my contract signing and that I needed to have my luggage packed and ready to go in thirty minutes. She gave me a hairdryer and I rushed back upstairs.

I dried my hair in the front bathroom and pictured my meeting with the owner of my apartment building, Dominik, and my moose. A locksmith had been called, and amazingly, he was there in ten minutes. I managed to get dressed properly for the occasion after all, pack everything I owned back into my substantial luggage, and drag it all downstairs just in time to meet Dominik, and off we went.

After the contracts were signed and the details were discussed, we were finished. I signed a three-year lease, shook hands, and Gerard handed me my keys. I felt so small as I sat on the floor alone. I realized that I had accomplished my first of many goals. Finding my own place in a new country. This empty flat had a long way to go to become my furnished home. I could only contemplate the many adventures that lay ahead of me.

MAGDY

I spent the first couple of nights in my new flat on a bed that I bought from a discount store. It actually was just the mattress, because the frame broke before they were able to deliver it to me.

I decided to go to IKEA and find something decent. Not sure how difficult it would be to get there; I hailed the first cab I saw. "Ich mochte nach IKEA, bitte." I would like to go to IKEA, please. I had been practicing German on my own. I would ask strangers who spoke English how to say something in German, and then I would write it down phonetically. The driver, Magdy, was a joyful, inquisitive man in his early forties with dark skin, slicked-back black hair and a big smile, but he spoke very little English, and I spoke even less German. He said, "My name is Magdy, and I am from Egypt." We communicated as best we could. I managed to explain to him that because his taxi was a large van, it would be great if he could pick me up when I was finished shopping. I planned to have too much to carry for a smaller taxi. He gave me his phone number and dropped me off at the entrance to Ikea.

I find IKEA stores to be hard to navigate in the States, but when everything is in German, well now, that's a whole new level! After about an hour and a half, I finally matched the right-sized mattress to the right-sized frame to the right-sized sheets at the most affordable price. I called Magdy, and when he picked me up he said he would help carry all of my heavy stuff upstairs to my flat. It worked out great. The cost of delivery for most stores was ninety euros. Magdy just left his meter running, so the delivery worked out to be three euros. Little did he know that over the next two months he would be taking me to outdoor flea markets and antique stores, and helping me carry still more heavy things up the stairs!

Later that week, I found a nice little desk in an antique store in Hauptplatz. After I paid for it, I called Magdy and handed the phone to the salesgirl. She gave Magdy directions to the store, and within ten minutes, he was there to help me load the desk and carry it up to my flat. Together we made a great team.

Christina came to visit me shortly after I moved in, and we went to an open-air flea market. We found a beautiful kitchen table. It was at least one hundred years old and hand-carved. We managed to carry it to the curb and noticed that a lot of people were stopping to look at our purchase. One woman stopped long enough for me to ask her why people were taking such an interest in this table. She told us that this was a very special Austrian antique and we were lucky to have it.

I called Magdy and he loaded up our lucky find. My flat, thanks in part to this wonderfully helpful stranger, really was starting to feel like a home.

I NEED A SCREWDRIVER

When I took everything I had bought out of the IKEA boxes, I thought, "I can do this." What was going to be my new full-size bed looked like a stack of kindling and odd road maps. There were drawings of stick figures with happy faces completing their projects, but given the complicated do-it-my-own-damn-self IKEA task in front of me, my face did not look like theirs. I got as far as I could when I realized that I couldn't go any further without a screwdriver.

My flat was in downtown Graz, so I went in search of a hardware store. I asked a few people who didn't speak English, and they pointed to a side street. I walked in that direction for ten minutes when I saw a man wearing a tool belt who looked to be in his thirties standing in front of an old commercial building. He had dark curly hair, beautiful brown skin, and dark brown eyes. I asked him if he spoke any English, and he smiled and said, "a little." I showed him my IKEA drawing of a screwdriver, and he said that if I went twenty minutes in the opposite direction, I would find the Austrian version of a Home Depot. He also said that if I could wait for one hour, he would come over and help me build it! He was doing some repairs on the building in front of us and was headed to the store to get something to drink. He invited me to go with him to the market.

We walked together, talking about life in Graz. His name was Daniel, and he was from Romania. Daniel, as it turned out, had managed to find some work doing small construction jobs and was working for cash under the table. He was sharing a small flat with a female friend that had also moved from Romania. I thought it was sweet that when we were in the store he bought us each an iced tea, and then he went back to work while I headed for the hardware store.

Daniel and I agreed to meet in front of the building he was working on in about an hour. At the hardware store, I bought a screwdriver, a level, some nails, and a small hammer. When I returned to his building, my new handyman was standing outside waiting for me. I was a little surprised. I think that my faith in mankind at that point in my life was low. I trusted people but I didn't trust they'd be there for me when they said they would.

Back at my place, Daniel started to assemble the pile of rubble that was to be my bed. When I asked him how I could help, he said, "Just tell me stories about America!" His accent was enjoyable to listen to, and he sounded Italian. So while following his lead on the IKEA project, I told him what life was like for me in California. In the US things are different. At least where I was from, life was made easier by modern conveniences. Moving to Graz, I told him, was a big challenge for me.

Daniel, in turn, shared that he wasn't happy with his current living arrangements. He and his roommate fought a lot and he really needed more income. He didn't have any friends, and even though he had been in Graz for seven years, it was difficult for him to socialize. He had a happy personality and seemed like he would be fun to hang out with, so I told him, "I will be your friend!" We both smiled.

It took Daniel and me almost three hours to complete the bed because we had to build the box spring one stick at a time. When we were finished, I tried to pay him for his help, but he refused. We agreed that I could take him to lunch sometime the following week, and we exchanged phone numbers. I got my bed built and made a friend simply because I walked down some random street! Sometimes successful outcomes in life owe everything to meticulous planning, and sometimes it's just a matter of serendipity.

STORAGE

I had a great night's sleep on my new bed, and in the morning I was wondering what to do with the other mattress I had bought. It was a large twin-size that would be perfect if Kevin and Christina were both staying with me at the same time. I had a great couch that folded out to a bed for one, and this other mattress would fit nicely in the large entryway inside my flat. And so the endless process of "accumulating more stuff" had begun -- it's a constant in life; it seems, even for the traveler. Now what to do with the extra mattress during the day when I didn't need it?

In search of an answer to that pressing question, I ventured down into the bowels of my glorious old building to see what I could find. My building is hard to explain, but I will try. It was completely enclosed like a hotel, but the hallways and large, wide staircases were cold concrete with small arched windows and an occasional random ornate sink. I went to the bottom level, which was mostly underground. There were rustic wood and iron-framed windows that let in very little daylight. I walked down a dark hallway and was struggling to see until I found a light switch. When I turned it on, there was a light bulb hanging from a wire that barely lit up a dirt floor and revealed small storage units divided by very old pieces of wood and wire. It looked like an underground stable from a thousand years ago! Each unit was about 4 x 6 ft. and had a gate with a lock on each one. One had some boxes stored in it, and another contained some old tools and broken furniture, but they all were locked. The place gave me a minor case of the creeps, but as anyone who has ever felt pinched for space in a home or an apartment knows, you don't turn down storage!

I went back upstairs and called my realtor to see if perhaps one of these dungeons belonged to my apartment. He didn't answer; so I went back down to have another look. This time, in the darkness, I noticed rusted brass numbers on each storage gate. My apartment unit number was five. I saw the number one, next to that two, then three, four, but no five? They stopped at eight. I checked to see if somehow I could shove a mattress into one of them, but I could tell that wasn't going to work.

I walked away from that hallway and noticed that in the opposite direction there was a large wooden plank door. It stood alone and looked like something out of a Steven King movie. As I turned to leave, I saw a rusty number five hanging on the door. No way!

There was a lock on the door, so I ran upstairs to get my set of keys. When I returned, my key fit the lock, and the door opened! Inside was a dirt floor, and there was a small window at the top made of wood and metal bars like an old jail. The ceiling was high and arched like a tunnel. It had its own light that lit up the room better than the other storage units. There were metal shelves along one wall and some noteworthy medieval-looking hooks on another. This place was ten times larger than the other ones, and all the walls were exposed brick. Well, the old place had coughed up one of its secrets, and I had found my very own cavernous storage dungeon.

GIGGLES

The following day was beautiful. I walked through the city where the architecture was breathtaking. It looked like the quintessential European city. Each storefront was different from the next. Small tables lined the streets with red umbrellas providing shade. I saw a man on one corner playing a saxophone, and farther up the street was a young man playing his guitar and singing. The streets were always full of live music. I passed people sitting by a fountain drinking Prosecco and eating colorful desserts. Later I would find out that most of the architecture was of Italian design because Italians helped Graz rebuild after the war. It was sunny and warm, and the people there had suffered a long, cold winter. I could feel their delight in the fresh spring air, and felt it just as strongly myself.

I enjoyed my leisurely stroll back home and then checked my phone for messages. I saw that Daniel, who helped me build my bed, had called three times. Just as I was about to return his call, he called again. His voice was excited and urgent, and his diction took on the rather stilted quality that high passion sometimes lends a person's speech: "Diane, I can't stop thinking about you!" His accent made the call sound like something out of a movie, as he continued, "Diane, I don't know what has happened to me! Usually I am the one who is distant, but I can't help myself. What have you done to me? I am crazy for you!" I thought, "What the hell is this?" He sounded like he was losing his mind. I told him that I preferred to date older men, whereas he was only in his thirties. Daniel insisted that he must be part of my life, even if it was just as friends. "Promise me that we will be friends forever! Promise me this!" His voice was getting even more earnest. I said in a tone that must have sounded more like a question to him than a declaration, "Okay, we will be friends forever?" "Swear this to me! You don't understand. The women here are closed and you are so open and genuine! You will see how they are, you will see. Please swear to me!"

While I wasn't lacking in empathy, all the same I couldn't help but giggle just for a moment. This grown man was losing it over me, and we had only spent a few hours together. I didn't even look good that day. In fact, the day we met, I was wearing a dirty sweatshirt, jeans, and no makeup. Truth be told, I looked pretty bad. So here I was in this beautiful place on a perfect day listening to a young fellow tell me that he couldn't live without me!

I calmed him down and told him that we would be friends and spend some "friend time" together. I told him that we could run errands or maybe have lunch sometime. I knew better than to agree to dinner where wine might be involved. He sounded better after I made this promise, and we agreed to talk later in the week. After that he called me at least once a week. I would have short polite conversations with him, but I didn't want to encourage his infatuation. I never saw him in person again. It's not that there was anything wrong with Daniel it's just that I was focused on setting up my new life. I had tunnel vision and all I could see was how much I still had to accomplish before I could call Graz my home. The next few weeks when ever Daniel would call we would talk about everyday difficulties. He couldn't find an adequate job and I couldn't find where to pay my utility bills. He wanted more friends to hang out with and I just wanted to know why my cell phone wouldn't call Ireland. Finally time passed and my admirer faded away, which, given the circumstances, I think was best.

ACCLIMATED

few weeks later, I was awakened by bright sunlight flooding through
my window. The blue sky was adorned with delicate white clouds,
and I could smell the flowers even with my window closed. This looked
to be the perfect day to catch up on mundane tasks like laundry, grocery shopping, and housecleaning. After my morning coffee I tried to get
dressed and out the door, but for some reason I felt lazy. I sat around all
morning trying to get myself motivated to do something, anything at all,
with no success. I finally gave in to it, and while in bed eating chocolates,
I managed to watch four hours of *The Sopranos*. Hating that I was wasting
the day, I got up, got dressed, and joined the people who were enjoying
their Saturday afternoon walking around Graz's city center.

I was in a zombie-like state. I shuffled into a large shoe store and tried
on fifteen pairs of shoes. I then schlepped into a coffee store and drank
their free samples. Passing by a park with energetic kids running around
only pointed out my lack of energy. I passed by my drycleaners without
my dirty laundry, so there was no need to go in. After that, I walked down
an alley I had never seen before. I passed through a huge enclosed stone
hallway, and then into an enormous courtyard. I found myself completely

surrounded by large, ornate buildings, columns, and archways. The ground and the buildings were constructed of beige-colored stone. Everything was the same light color.

The large center of this impressive courtyard was completely empty except for a red fabric-draped couch! The couch itself wasn't empty: two people were sitting on it, relaxing. Over a loudspeaker echoing through the courtyard was a recording of a woman's voice speaking in German.

I walked around for a few minutes, feeling confused, when I noticed that now there was only one person sitting on the couch. It was a woman in her early forties, and she motioned for me to come join her. I walked over and sat down. "You are not Austrian, are you?" she asked. I said no, and asked her what was going on. The speech blaring through the speaker was so loud that I had to lean in close to hear her explanation: "Tomorrow is Labor Day, so today is the Day of Laziness." Well, I suppose that's one way of putting it, though the history of Labor Day is hardly about "idleness" in a detrimental sense.

She said that these were government buildings surrounding us and that she thought this was the perfect place to display her red couch to encourage people to sit and relax. I asked her, "What does the government think of you using their courtyard for your demonstration?" She just smiled and said, "Today they are closed!" I thanked her for sharing with me, and went on my way. I came across a small parade of people who were acting out a funeral procession. I could tell that they were making some kind of statement about the non-labor day. After the parade passed, I saw some young people giving out free soup and bread.

The day was about supporting the idea that people need to take time off from work and enjoy more free time. How ironic is that? I was celebrating their holiday before I even knew it existed. I guess I was starting to acclimate.

#@*!%*#!

I hired a handyman to help me hang a recent purchase of dark navy blue velvet drapes, which were a lavish twelve feet in length. My usual taste in décor was contemporary/eclectic, but because I was starting a new life in a new world, I really wanted to embrace the polar opposite. The handyman was from Bosnia and had such a long name that he just went by Mickey. His accent was pretty thick, but he spoke English and we managed to communicate well enough. I had the rod and hardware and had borrowed a ladder from the dungeon downstairs. When he assessed the situation, he said that what I needed was luck. I asked why I needed luck and he explained. Apparently, this building was close to one hundred years old. He said that the walls were filled with rocks. "Rocks?" I asked. He then drilled into the wall and with a lot of struggle and cursing, he pulled out a rock. It was the size of an almond. I then asked, "How will I ever hang anything?" He responded, "Luck!" Now there's an interior design principle you can take to the bank, right?

We got everything ready and the drilling began. With the drilling came a lot of cursing: "#$@!&*)*%!" Then a new hole had to be drilled, which brought forth a fresh rant. I didn't mind the swearing, but it made me feel like the job I gave him was miserable. I really wanted my glorious drapes to be hung, so I just stayed out of it. It took almost an hour, but soon they were up and beautiful. I said to him, "I love them! My flat looks like a castle!" To that he responded, "And you are the princess! Give me twenty euros!"

A month later, I had Mickey come over to hang a light in my kitchen and then a small chandelier in my bathroom. Again he started in with, "@#%!*>. . . *&%#@!" I said, "I'm sorry my projects are so frustrating for you." He turned around with a puzzled look on his face and asked me why I thought he was frustrated. I said that with all of his cursing, he must have been having a difficult time. He shook his head and said, "No, not difficult, is no problem!" Then he went back to his work and his cursing with equal concentration.

Alrighty then!

ONE CHANDELIER TO GO

Summer had arrived and Christina came for another visit. We both loved to decorate living spaces so we spent most of the day shopping. We found a few different antique shops that had some chandeliers, but they were all over one thousand euro, and that was for the cheap ones. We moved on to other things like rugs and a coffeemaker and were satisfied with our purchases.

By the end of the day, we were both in the mood for some Indian cooking. Using the Internet we found a place nearby called Ganesha. We walked a few blocks from my flat to the entrance. It was painted bright yellow and had an open door leading straight downstairs to the underground dining room. The small restaurant was pretty full, but we got a nice table. The walls were also painted yellow and adorned with brightly colored scarves and family photos of India. I couldn't help but notice the absolutely perfect chandelier hanging above the center of the room. Christina and I both agreed that we needed to find one just like that! It was about 10 p.m. and the owner asked if we could order before the kitchen closed. We got a nice bottle of wine and some great curry dishes. The owner introduced himself. "Hello! My name is Sathi!" He was an extremely jovial man in his forties who had moved to Austria from India eleven years ago. When we finished our dinner, Sathi brought over three shot glasses with mango Schnapps and sat down to drink. The restaurant had only a few customers left, so he was free to join us. An inquisitive man, he wanted to know where we were from and how we ended up in Graz. I told him my story and then asked about his. He said that he wanted a better life for his family, so he studied the German language, saved up enough money to open a restaurant and chose Graz for the same reasons I did. Christina had been to India, so she and Sathi talked about the relaxed lifestyle in India, and the different foods served in different regions. For example, some parts are known for their vegetarian food and others for unique flavors and seasonings. Christina's visit to India involved attending a wedding ceremony, so they talked about the use of henna tattoos and the long process of getting ready for an Indian wedding.

The other patrons had gone and a couple of employees were left cleaning the kitchen. The three of us talked for over an hour until we were the only ones left in the building. I felt privileged to sit at the table with the owner and talk as if we were old friends. "I really love your chandelier, it's beautiful! Where did you get it?" I asked. "I brought it here from India eleven years ago. It is yours!" he said. "No way!" I exclaimed. "I could never accept something so precious, but thank you!"

Sathi smiled and said, "I insist -- I can tell that you will appreciate this gift, and I was going to buy a new one anyway." Christina and I looked at each other in disbelief and smiles. "Well then, you must let me buy a new one for you," I said. Sathi said that it wasn't necessary, and it was settled. I would be able to pick up the chandelier next month.

It was one in the morning when Christina and I helped Sathi close the restaurant for the night. We washed glasses, folded cloth napkins and set the tables for the next day. We grabbed our belongings, and he offered to drive us home. In front of my building, the three of us stood under the black night sky and dim streetlights. We talked a little more and agreed that we would keep in touch and visit at his restaurant often.

JUST ANOTHER
DAY IN GRAZ

With Christina back in Ireland I found myself alone again. I was surprised that I never felt lonely. I had frequent communication with all of my family so I never felt homesick. Everyday I found a different street to discover and enjoyed doing it on my own. On this particular day I found myself walking through my favorite place, Hauptplatz. I was hungry and decided to stop and have lunch at an outdoor café next to a gorgeous fountain. The weather was warm and the blue sky was breath taking. I ordered lunch, a salad with grilled chicken and an iced tea. When two young women heard me speaking English to the waitress, they introduced themselves. "Hallo, we are Christine and Dominika." They asked me where I was on holiday from, and I told them that I had moved to Graz from California. Then they asked the same second question I got over and over: "Had you ever been to Graz before?" When I answered, "I've never been to Graz before, and sold everything I owned to move here to start a new life," they gave me the same look I got in Europe over and over! Everyone was always surprised that an American woman would take on a new country sight unseen. Why was this? I wondered at the time, and still wonder. What's the underlying assumption -- is it about American women in particular, or are most people afraid to move far away from where they grew up?

The two young women invited me to join them at their table. Christine was twenty-two and spoke enough English to get by. Dominika was thirty-two and didn't speak any English. I could tell that they were close, and I asked if they were dating each other. They said yes, and that initiated our conversation about the differences between the U.S. and Europe. They asked if gay people were accepted in the U.S., and I said it depends on whom you ask. They said they didn't have any problems with it in Europe. At least in Austria, no one gave much thought to sexual preferences. We enjoyed our iced tea and sunshine, and they brought up the idea of going to a *Buschenshänke* sometime in the near future. I had heard about them but hadn't been to one. A *Buschenshänke* is a place to drink wine and eat food that is produced on that particular property. They follow regulations mandating that only cold food and homemade pastries can be served. The typical fare consists of cold cuts -- for example, smoked meat, roast pork, ham, dry sausage and spreads including bacon jam, liver pâté, pumpkin seed spread and horseradish. All of this, including an assortment of breads, is served on a large wooden platter. Buschenshänke are located in beautiful vineyards and lush countryside's. Each one is required to serve only products that they have grown and prepared themselves.

We did meet again. On a visit that included my daughter and son, the five of us actually went to a Buschenshänke. Christine and Dominika picked us up in their car, and we drove for forty minutes through green countryside to a wooden cabin-like structure in a vineyard. We sat inside of what looked like a combination farmhouse and winery at a picnic table. There we were served platter after platter of cheeses, meats, fruits, breads and pâté. The food kept coming until we were more than full. All of this cost the equivalent of a McDonalds Happy Meal!

After my initial meeting with Christine and Dominika at the outdoor café, I went home to meet my handyman Mickey for some more light installations.

In the bathroom, a light bulb hung from the ceiling, and there were some exposed electrical wires above the mirror for additional lighting. I had bought two bathroom lights from IKEA. Mickey and I hung one from the ceiling and one above the mirror, all the while teaching each other how to say dirty words in our native languages. He also spoke fluent German. He wanted to know how to say general four-letter words in English, but what I wanted to know there was no equivalent for in German. The word was "jerk." I said that sometimes someone isn't so bad that I would use the word "asshole," but I needed a word that was belittling. It turns out that in the German language there aren't many "middle of the road words": things are great or despicable, mean or nice, good or bad. They don't have something in between like "jerk." I had even asked Dominik the hotel manager this same question and he came up with "nose picker." I didn't know what to do with that one!

Finished with our electrical work, Mickey hit the switch and both lights came on. When we turned it off, only one went off. There wasn't any way to turn the one above the mirror off. After agreeing that I needed a new outlet, we had to leave things in that unsatisfactory state: whenever I had to turn off the lights, I would need to use the electrical breaker in the entryway. Complications! I felt a bit like uttering some of the dirty words I had taught Mickey, but there was nothing to be done for it at the moment. At least hanging the lighting fixtures was progress of a sort.

Dinner that night was excellent! I went to visit Sathi the restaurateur, with whom I had by then become even more of a friend than a culinary patron, and while we ate together, he gave me German lessons. I started to notice that when I spoke the words I learned from Sathi, I said them with an Indian accent. When I spoke the words I learned from Mickey, I had a Bosnian accent, and as for the words I got from Magdy, I sounded Arabic.

I was indeed "learning German," as a relatively long-term visitor should, but all the same, I was a veritable Pu Pu platter of *die Deutsche Sprache!* I wonder if it's that way with other strangers in a strange land: is perfect command of a new language just an impossible dream? Does it matter? I mean, isn't it one of the most delightful things about interacting with people from elsewhere that you get to hear your language spoken in interesting new ways, "correctness" be damned?

PIZZA, ANYONE?

I enjoyed many different culinary delights in Graz. Within walking distance from my flat I found Spanish, Chinese, Russian, French and Italian. My challenge was traditional pizza. There were plenty of great Italian restaurants with good salads and pasta. The problem was trying to translate the American version of pepperoni pizza to the Austrian. The first time I ordered a pepperoni pizza, I got a cheese pizza with yellow chili peppers all over it. I asked the waiter about the yellow stuff on my pizza, and he said that there wasn't anything on my pizza but cheese. Hmmm...

The next time I went to an Italian restaurant, I saw a guy eating a pizza with the same yellow chili peppers all over it, and I asked the waiter what was on that pizza. He said cheese and paprika. Okay, so next time I would say "kein Paprika," no paprika.

One night around nine-thirty, I wanted a pepperoni pizza. I had a flyer that was left on my door for free delivery. I could tell by the address that it was nearby. I called and asked if anyone spoke English, but no luck. I saw one possibility that looked safe, a Hawaiian pizza. The ingredients were in German, but how can you go wrong with Hawaiian?

It took only twenty-five minutes for the deliveryman to show up at my door. Cool! I paid the six euros plus a small tip and skipped inside. As I was skipping, I smelled fish. What? No way, I hate all fish! I opened the box and saw a pizza covered in squid or octopus. Disgusting! It seems that to the pizza place I bought from, "Hawaiian" meant "seafood." I had to get that horrid box out of my apartment, quick. I didn't want to waste it, and knew that someone else might think a pizza that smelled like a boat dock in a dirty marina was perfection. I went outside and looked at the front of my building for anyone who had his or her lights on. It was now 10 p.m. I saw that the lights for the apartment at the opposite end of my hall were on, and I remembered that two nuns lived there.

I took the smelly box to their door and heard voices coming from inside their apartment. I knocked on the door, and the woman who answered spoke only German. I didn't know how to say anything like this in German, so I used facial expressions and hand gestures to illustrate my displeasure for this pizza and my hopes that they might enjoy it. The mime act worked. I opened the box and showed her the mess; she smiled and nodded her head. She took the pizza inside and from outside the closed door I could hear two women laughing. I found out later that they enjoyed the pizza!

Great is the power of pizza. Not entirely put off by my unfortunate "squid pie" experience, I went back inside, still wanting to succeed in my quest. I called the restaurant again, and this time I said in English, "Don't you have a pepperoni pizza?" The woman on the other end of the phone said, "absolutely." In twenty-five minutes, the same deliveryman was at my door.

He looked a little confused, and using facial expression, hand gestures, and some German; I explained to him what had happened. He understood me and wanted to give me the second pizza for free. I said no, this was my fault, and I was learning. I took the box inside and ate my cheese pizza with yellow chili peppers.

42

Later, I talked to Christina online and told her about my struggle. She looked up, "Americans looking for pizza in Graz," on her computer and said that the website she found stated, "Americans looking for pizza the way they want it in Graz is a challenge!" It turns out that pepperoni in Graz is *pepperoncini*. If you want pepperoni, then you need to order salami, and you will never find cheese that is similar to what you would find in the States. That's correct, at least in my experience. Graz pizza apparently doesn't get sprinkled with mozzarella.

Well, my pizza adventures taught me something about traveling to far-away places: you really can't take much for granted or put even seemingly common experiences in the "universal" bin. Something as straightforward and delightful as pizza is fraught with hazards for your taste buds and your sense of culinary right and wrong. The stuff turns out to be almost as variable as language itself. *Guten Appetit! Ich lerne. . .* I'm learning!

CHRISTIAN

When I signed the rental agreement for my flat, the rental agent told me that I needed to go to a government building to register. When anyone moves to Austria, they must let the authorities know, present their passport, and fill out some forms. I am not really sure what it is all about. I just know that it is mandatory. I had been putting it off because I didn't want to take the time to figure out where this building was. The address I was given was incomplete, so I set out in the direction of town where it would most likely be. I finally found it.

When I got there, I saw that the inside resembled a typical DMV in the States. I took a number and got in line behind twenty other people. There were posters on the walls with what looked like health warnings and important dates to remember. One of them had a picture of a tic-like bug and a girl walking on crutches. Based on my translation, they had ticks in Austria, and if you were bitten, you could end up crippled.

I looked through my documents and had filled out the required forms weeks before with some help from my realtor, Gerard. They wanted to know my new address, birth date, country of origin, etc. When it came to the box where you declare your religion, I left it blank. Usually, in the States, this is optional.

When it was my turn, I sat down in front of a middle-aged woman who spoke only German. I gave her the forms, and after a few minutes, she looked confused. She held out my papers and pointed to the empty box regarding religion. She pushed the paper back towards me and pointed her finger sternly at the empty box. I looked at it, and in the provided space, I wrote "Christian." She didn't recognize this term because it is different in German. Again she abruptly pushed the form back to me and pointed to the religion box. I didn't know why this was so important, but apparently we weren't moving on until the matter was resolved.

We both tried to communicate in our respective languages, but obviously this wasn't getting us anywhere. The woman finally turned her computer monitor towards me, and I could see some sort of list. It was all in German, and she wanted me to choose one. "Ok, how about this one?" I pointed to something on the screen. She looked at me with her eyebrows raised and shook her head. I didn't recognize any of these words, so maybe I had picked something that seemed very unlikely to her. I tried again. I saw one option that the first word started with an "R" and the second word started with a "C." Maybe this was Roman Catholic? Or maybe it was . . . well, how could I be sure? I went with it and pointed to the screen. She looked at my new choice and smiled and nodded her head in approval. After a few minutes of going through the rest of my paperwork, she looked up and said that I had passed. Wow, I didn't realize that this was something I could fail!

A GOOD FRIDAY

It was another sunny Friday afternoon in Graz. I walked to the city center and found an intriguing restaurant I hadn't noticed before. It was called Café Sacher, and it looked very regal. There were a few tables outside, but the tunnel-like entrance had a narrow red carpet down the center and I couldn't wait to look inside. I thought it might be a private club based on the red velvet rope adjacent to the hostess desk. Either way I was seated. In the center of the room was an ornate planter filled with flowers and plants. Surrounding the planter was a circular sofa in rich red fabric. The room was lit by the sunlight flooding in through the atrium windows two stories above. As I sipped my tea and looked around the room, I noticed a table with three women in their late seventies, all dressed up and wearing pearls. I loved watching them enjoy their lunch together. They were very elegant, and every subtle gesture or movement of their hands seemed to be posed and thought out. I tried not to stare, but I found them mesmerizing. Looking at the menu I was surprised at how inexpensive everything was. I ordered a small salad, a chicken dish and an ice coffee. The waiter told me that the restaurant was famous for its Sacher torte, and if I came back, I should try it. When my ice coffee came I was speechless. Before me was an old fashioned ice cream parlor glass stuffed with three scoops of vanilla ice cream and a pile of whipped cream on top. Protruding from the top of it all was a mini paper parasol with a plastic monkey hanging from it. This looked more like a dessert for two than a coffee. I later learned that ice in German means ice cream.

After lunch, I walked down one of the many random alleys in the area, and it opened up into a courtyard with more cafés and shops. I saw a traditional Austrian restaurant and decided to check it out for future dining. It was really nice inside. I walked through a room with wrought-iron lanterns hanging from the ceiling and dark wood floors. Then, it was down two steps into another room with great antique tables and chairs. There was one room after another, each just a little more interesting than the one before. One had dark green walls, a fireplace and six tables for four. It had the look of a hunting lodge. Another had picnic tables and colorful tile floors that gave it a Spanish feel. I saw a staircase that led up to rooftop seating with all sorts of umbrellas and candles everywhere. There, a waiter approached me and I said, "*Ich schaue nur, danke,*" which I used a lot. It means, "I'm just looking, thank you." Indeed I was. I sat down at the bar downstairs and enjoyed a glass of Prosecco while looking through some Graz tourism information I had picked up earlier.

This was a day of just strolling along and intently observing the life happening around me in the city, catching little moments before they disappeared.

Leaving the restaurant, I heard some music coming from another courtyard and I decided to take a look. There was a temporary open-air market with arts and crafts available for purchase and a live band playing gypsy music. I stopped for a while to listen, and a lady wearing a belly dancing costume came out of nowhere and started to dance wildly in front of the band. I could tell by the reaction of the band members that they had no idea who this woman was! She danced around with her purse on her shoulder and her sweater in her hand. The people in the crowd looked like they thought she was crazy.

I took my time as I strolled along the arts and crafts booths, stopping here and there. One caught my attention. There was a casually dressed man painting a field of flowers on a large canvas. I watched him taking his time brushing on the final touches of a beautiful blue sky. On the ground at his feet was a young boy playing with a little puppy. That sight looked like a painting in itself. The woman seated next to them looked to be the boy's mother. I struck up a conversation with the young family by asking about the artwork. The booth was filled with beautiful oil paintings of flowers and landscapes. I especially liked one that had a field of blue and yellow flowers with white clouds above. I asked how much it was, and the price was reasonable, so I bought it. His wife took the painting over to the easel so her husband could touch up a flaw she saw at the top. The boy didn't speak English, but he smiled and wanted me to play with his dog. Together, we rolled a small red ball back and forth, much to the dog's delight. The boy's mother was dressed like a character out of *Little House on the Prairie.* Wearing an apron over a peasant dress, she wore no make-up and a very sweet face. She offered me a cup of tea while my painting dried. We talked about her husband's galleries in Vienna where his paintings cost three times as much. She said that he was well known there, and had come to Graz to introduce his artwork to a new city. He didn't speak much, but smiled at me when he handed me my purchase. I wondered how I was going to fit the 4 x 3-foot painting on the tram with me. I opted to walk it home, which was awkward but only took ten minutes. I hung it in my living room . . . beautiful! I enjoyed relating to art this way -- the painting was very fine in its own right, but it meant more to me as the culmination of my experiences on a day spent taking in the sights and sounds of a city now less foreign to me, but somehow still strange and wonderful in what it had to offer.

KAPUTT = BROKEN

A month or so had passed, and one day I was riding the tram back and forth all day long running errands. It was 1.90 euro for each one-hour ticket. They run on the honor system, and you never know when the tram police will show up and charge you a fine if you don't have a ticket. I always had my ticket at the ready. That day I was using the onboard ticket machine, trying to purchase a ticket for one week. It got a little confusing, and as I struggled with the ticket options, I realized that we had reached my stop. I thought, "No worries, I will get it next time."

I should have known what was coming next: after all, Murphy's Law applies just as much in Graz as it does anywhere else. No doubt it extends across the universe. Just as I turned to walk off the tram, two women in plain clothing approached me asking to see my ticket. I said, "This is my stop, can we talk outside?" They escorted me off the tram, and they didn't speak any English at all. I used all the German I had learned up to this point. "Ich versuche Gehirn kaputt." This is how it translated: "I trying, brain broken." They looked at each other and said to me, "sixty euro." I looked around for someone to translate, but no luck. I tried to explain again: "From USA . . . new in Graz . . brain is broken for ticket machine."

49

I'm not sure what was more embarrassing -- skipping out on my ticket and getting caught, or having my limited German language skills put on public display in an unfriendly context!

Again they said, "sixty euro." Fine. I showed them that I only had fifty euro on me. They took my cell phone from me, and I understood when they motioned for me to go home and get the rest. I did just that, and when I gave them the full amount, they returned my cell phone. The next day I figured out how to buy long-term tickets, so no harm done.

My troubles with "tech" didn't end there, unfortunately. Several days later, I was using my laptop in the morning when suddenly everything stopped working. The screen was full of urgent German words and warnings. Internet access was much cheaper for legal residents, so I paid a local friend to get it for me. I had to pay month to month and any information regarding my bill was in German. With what I could understand, I concluded that my access had run out. That didn't make much sense, because I had just paid it three days ago, and it usually lasted much longer than that. I am one of those people who drag their feet on learning new technology. Years ago I held on to my old flip phone until I was forced to get a new one because it was too antiquated for modern data. As far as computers go, I would only learn the minimal amount needed to communicate with my family through email and, eventually, Facebook. I headed out to the city center and found my Internet store. I brought my computer in so they could translate for me and I would understand next time. We figured it all out, and I left to run some errands.

I got a quick lunch, looked for an alarm clock, bought a hairdryer, and ended up in a clothing store looking at some great sale items. I found a nice pair of jeans and a couple of tops. As I headed for the register to pay, I saw that I no longer had my laptop. Shit! I ran to the dressing room, but it wasn't there. I looked every place I had stopped in the store, but couldn't find it. I ran to where I had eaten lunch, but my computer just wasn't there. I started to panic when I remembered that all of my banking information *and* all of my passwords were in my computer. Anyone could access my critical information, because I hadn't set up an Apple login password. Exhibit A: basic information security -- one of those things we tend to learn the hard way.

My eyes started to tear up -- I thought my life in Graz was over. If you've ever lost an item that was extremely important to you -- say, a pair of eyeglasses that you can scarcely see without; a cash-and-credit-card-filled wallet or an expensive watch, you'll understand the numb fright that I felt just then. All losses of that sort have some such effect on us, but some are more saturated with past anxieties or regrets than others. I had come to Graz to get a fresh look at life and renew myself. How could I go on if my bank accounts and identity were taken? Much of my remaining stay might be occupied with little but "damage control." Well, I checked everywhere twice and then thought maybe I had left the laptop at the Internet store. I ran in and the salesgirl said that it was not there, but then she pointed outside. What? She saw that I was in a state of panic and escorted me to the ATM machine next door. Next to that was a small room attached to a restaurant with some women cleaning vegetables. The salesgirl told these women that I had lost my computer and one of them promptly reached over to a table inside and handed it to me. I had left it at the ATM machine next door over an hour ago. Needless to say, I thanked my benefactors profusely. Often we have good reason to worry about other people's honesty, which only makes the genuine article all the more refreshing.

One helpful note in all this minor travail was that I found myself learning more Austrian German every day, and soon began to receive at least one compliment a day on my pronunciation. I was learning out of sheer necessity.

FLOWERS

One Friday, I went to listen to some live music playing at my favorite pub. For the past few weeks, I'd been running errands and spending my time alone. I hadn't put much effort into my appearance. Feeling unattractive for too long I spent extra time getting ready and hoped to feel better about myself. When I arrived at the pub, I saw a group of young guys playing a bar game that I hadn't seen before. There was a small, square box the size of a coaster on the bar. The bartender placed a tiny bottle of alcohol on the box, and a green light came on. The young man sitting across from him grabbed the bottle, unscrewed the cap, downed the alcohol, and placed the bottle back on the box. Then a red light came on. They looked at the box and the bartender wrote down his timed speed, keeping a running tally. Then it was the bartender's turn to try to beat that speed. This went on for a few rounds until a winner was declared. It looked fun, what with everyone cheering for them. I thought it was different and quirky compared to the usual drinking games in the states.

Eventually, these young men started to talk to me, and I asked them where they were from. They said that they lived half an hour train ride from Graz. Then they asked me questions about where I was from, what I was doing in Graz, and so forth: the usual things you get asked when you're a foreigner in a bar. At one point they asked how old I was, and I asked, "How old are you?" Most of them were in their early twenties. I thought it was cute that they had surrounded me and paid for my glass of wine. "How old do you think I am?" I asked. They agreed that I must be between thirty and thirty-five, and I just let it go at that. "The people have spoken!" as politicians say whenever it's the least bit convenient for them. Well, the truth is, I found it flattering that they didn't know I was fifty or that both of my kids were older than they were. Suddenly, I didn't feel unattractive anymore!

These fellows were really sweet, polite, and fun to talk to, though I can't recall what we talked about -- that was less memorable than the kindness they showed and the gestures they made. At one point, they all wanted their picture taken with me. We played a game of darts, and then a lady selling gorgeous long-stemmed red roses came into the pub. Each one of the boys grabbed their wallets and bought a rose, and one by one they each handed their roses to me. Six beautiful roses! An hour later, another lady came into the bar with lovely long-stemmed peach-colored roses. Again the boys grabbed their wallets, and again each one gave me another beautiful rose.

They asked if I wanted to go with them to the bar next door, and I thought, "Why not?" We were only at the next bar for about ten minutes when someone with lavender roses walked in, and before I could stop them, each young man handed me yet another rose.

Shortly after that, we called it a night. We walked outside, and I gave each one of them a hug goodbye and thanked them profusely for the pleasant night and the flowers.

I walked home with my pageant-worthy bouquet and a smile! Who says diamonds are a girl's best -friend, anyway?

SERIOUSLY?

One evening a few weeks later, I was having dinner alone at one of my favorite spots in Hauptplatz. I was just about to pay my bill when someone sent a glass of champagne over to my table. I looked around the room and saw two gentlemen and one woman raising their glasses in the air in my direction. I raised my glass towards them and initiated our "air toast." I was finished with my dinner, so I walked over to thank them and they insisted I join them.

The thirty-year-old woman at the table was Tunda from Romania. She had beautiful light-brown hair and a champagne-induced sparkle in her eyes. Andras was her Hungarian boyfriend, and the other man at the table was Hans. Hans was a heavyset, squinty-eyed Austrian attorney. He looked to be in his late fifties and had an abruptness in his deep, forced speech. Hans was wearing a suit perhaps coming straight from work. They appeared to be celebrating something and had had a few drinks. I couldn't get many answers because they were caught up in their boisterous conversation. The energy at the table was infectious! They were all talking over one another in several languages, and the laughter was loud enough to gain the attention of nearby tables. After a few minutes, they did their best to continue the evening speaking English. I answered their many questions about how I ended up in Graz and quickly observed that Tunda understood very little English.

After concluding their dinner portion of the evening, we headed off to a festive bar down the street. Seated outside under a star-filled sky, we continued our conversation: "We should all go boating in Croatia next weekend!" exclaimed Andras. "Yes! Whose boat do you want to take, mine or Hans's?" This question was directed towards me. "Are you inviting me?" I asked. "Yes! It will be magical," answered the group. I had never been to Croatia before, and this all sounded exciting. Hans and Andras discussed the pros and cons of each boat and decided that Han's boat would be the best choice. They explained to me that we would drive to the Marina in Krk and decide there whether we should sleep on the boat or stay in separate hotel rooms. I mentioned that I would require my own sleeping area, wherever that might be. It all sounded so exciting; discussing a future adventure with my new friends!

We exchanged phone numbers, and Tunda agreed to go shopping with me so I could have the appropriate attire for the trip. We agreed to meet at the previous restaurant the next day for lunch.

I waited for over an hour before Tunda showed up to our scheduled lunch. She didn't offer any apologies for her tardiness and was acting distracted. She quickly whisked me away to the nearest boutique. While shuffling through the clothing racks I struggled to communicate with Tunda. "Would this dress be nice for the boat?" I asked. She just smiled and shrugged her shoulders. "How about these white pants?" Again she brushed me off. Frustrated, I kept looking around and then she came up to me and asked, "Is no difference this boat or not?" What? Her English was worse than I had thought. I asked her, "Is this a casual place or do we dress nice?" She responded with "You make big something with no interest!" Hmmmmm.......

The weekend of our trip had arrived, and Hans called my cell phone. Speaking with people in broken English is hard enough in person, but on the phone it's even worse. "Diane! I there pick you up!" Did he mean now? I asked. He then asked, "You hear me yes?" I raised my voice as if that would help: "I'm home now -- are you at my home now?" He answered, "Ten minutes" Great! I was looking forward to my adventure. I had been thinking about it all week and even told my family and friends that I was going to Croatia. I was packed and ready to go two days prior. Outside, I saw Hans waving his hand in the air, calling me over to his car. I jumped in and he started driving. "When do we pick up Tunda and Andras?" I asked. "They not coming," he answered with his eyes staring straight ahead. "What do you mean they're not coming?" I was getting upset. "They do other things this weekend." Hans said sternly. My mind raced. I really wanted to go on this trip and had already bragged about it to everyone. Not hiding my shock and disappointment, I told Hans that this was unacceptable. He then abruptly stopped the car in the middle of the road and said, "You no wish to go, you no go. Is fine for me." I then felt extreme anger towards Tunda. Why hadn't she called me to at least try to tell me she wasn't going? Now the cranky Austrian and I are going? My plan was to hang out with Tunda, not Hans. I felt pressured to make a quick decision. My stubbornness got the best of me and I said to myself, screw it, I'm going. I would just make the best of it.

Hans and I drove for approximately four hours and passed through numerous passport checkpoints. He practiced his English and tried to help me with speaking German. I started to see a softer side of him. He was very patient helping me with my German vocabulary. He tried to teach me the history of the Austro-Hungarian Empire but I could only pick up bits and pieces. We stopped at a small village along the way and Hans bought me lunch. He was genuinely very thoughtful.

When we arrived at the Marina, Hans walked me over to his boat. Now, I'm not a boat snob, but I have owned a couple in my lifetime. I knew enough to know that this was not going to work for me. It was old, small, and smelled bad. "I'm not sleeping on this." I informed Hans. He looked puzzled, but told me that there was a hotel up the street we could stay the night in and see the beautiful sights of Croatia during the day.

In the hotel lobby, Hans and the people running the front desk were speaking only Croatian. The place was small, kind of bed-and-breakfast style without the breakfast. No one spoke any English. I had to take Hans's word for it when he said that there was only one room left. I could feel my face turning red with anger. I blurted out, "I'm not sleeping with you, and that, you'd better understand!"

He shrugged his shoulders as if he was just putting up with me. In the hotel room, I was glad to see there were two beds separated by a night-stand. I locked myself in the bathroom and tried to conjure up a better attitude. I wanted to see Croatia, and here was someone who knew everything about it and was willing to be my tour guide. He seemed harmless, and I believed that if push came to shove I could take him. He really acted as if he didn't care what I did.

We met up with a brother of his and a friend for dinner in town. Krk is the capital city of the Island of Krk. That is where I saw beautiful architecture, a castle on the sea, and glorious stone streets lined with tiny shops and places to eat. The four of us went to dinner at a place where mostly locals meet up. It was odd sitting at a table where my only communication was with Hans because, again, only Croatian was spoken. Hans's brother, who looked to be about forty-five, stared at me the entire evening. The three men talked amongst themselves about God knows what, and from the way they were looking at me, I'm sure my presence was part of that discussion. I just smiled and ate my dinner.

Back at the hotel, Hans and I had a glass of wine at the bar and then went up to the room. I locked myself in the bathroom, brushed my teeth, and decided on wearing jeans and a sweatshirt to bed.

I woke up the next morning happy that Hans hadn't tried anything during the night. We went to breakfast and spent the rest of the day sight-seeing. Croatia had many landscapes to explore. We saw hills of gray rocks with no vegetation that looked more like a moonscape than an earthly landscape. Then, just two miles away, there was a lush beach surrounded by trees and waterfalls. Beyond that was desert, and next we were on sand paths between sprawling hedges that channeled traffic to the shore.

All I could think about was how I wanted to come back someday with my kids and have a really good time on my terms!

Hans was a perfect gentleman the entire time, and even paid for everything. On our last day we drove to Graz by way of Italy. We had lunch in a border town near some Italian ruins, but I couldn't understand Hans well enough to know where we were.

Hans dropped me at my flat and I thanked him for everything. We actually became friends and met up a few times during the following months for drinks. Tunda, on the other hand, I will never forgive. She had my phone number and she should have tried harder to let me know she wasn't coming. Had I known sooner, I wouldn't have gone.

ONE NIGHT IN A BAR

A month had passed and day-by-day I was gradually feeling like a local. I was out running errands early in the evening, and I thought a beer sounded nice. I passed a tiny Irish pub and stepped inside. The pubs in Graz are a great place to meet up with friends or pop in alone. I would never go to a bar alone in California. I felt awkward eating alone in a restaurant there. I would pretend to look at my phone, dig through my purse, read the menu, anything to look busy. It was a rare occasion for someone to invite me into their conversation. That was not the case in Graz. More often than not, within minutes of my entering a pub or restaurant, I would be involved in some interesting conversation with other patrons. I guess you could say that the pubs in Graz really are a little like the TV show *Cheers*. I sat down at the bar and struck up a conversation with Valentin the bartender. In Graz, all the Irish pubs have English-speaking employees. This was something I really appreciated after a long day of struggling with the German language. After about an hour, two guys walked in, and quickly the four of us were drinking German beer and talking. Tony was a young guy from New Jersey and had been living in Graz for six years. He spoke perfect German, but with a Jersey accent. I found that amusing, but kept it to myself. He was living with his girlfriend and worked as a conductor on a train. Rhys was from London and had been living in Graz running his own flooring company. I guessed him to be forty years old. He had a permanent grin on his face that matched his cheerful personality. His grandmother had lived in Graz, and when she died she left her house to Rhys.

After a few beers, we started playing darts. More people had trickled in, and the atmosphere was lively. There was a four-foot-tall tree trunk near the door where men took turns hammering in nails and the quickest was the winner.

There were lots of goofy bar games to play, including one that involved a plastic crocodile. There was a TV screen above the bar that rotated photos of the locals having fun and enjoying live music. So I suppose if you weren't already having fun you could at least watch other people enjoying their evening. But as it turned out, I wasn't in that fix.

The four of us (the bartender included) played darts, and much to everyone's surprise, I was winning! I have no idea why -- maybe I had less to drink than they did. We talked, laughed, drank, and played games until I finally announced that it was time for me to go home. Rhys and Tony agreed, and we walked out together. We exchanged phone numbers and went our separate ways. It's common for such meetings to be simultaneously partings, of course -- you exchange numbers with someone new to you, but it's somehow understood that the exchange is a formality. Well, that didn't turn out to be the case in this instance, but more on that later.

Walking down the dark streets back to my flat, I was still smiling about all the fun we had. I looked to see what time it was and couldn't believe that it was 4 a.m. How could I have been there for nine hours? I think the constant stimulation of a crowded bar combined with alcohol might have had something to do with it. Just when you think you are ready to leave, new people join in and the cycle of sharing the events of the day and a beer starts over again. The time just flies by!

HER COUNTRYMEN

Taking advantage of the warm summer weather, my kids scheduled another visit to Graz. The three of us took in the local sights. One evening, we went to visit my friend Sathi at his restaurant. We were greeted by Sathi's smiling face and hugs for everyone followed by great Indian food. At the end of our meal, Sathi joined us and we visited for a while. This was Sathi's first time meeting Kevin, so he was curious. "Where do you live? What do you think of your sister and mother living in foreign countries? Do you want to travel? Tell me everything!" Kevin said it was great that his mother had the courage to start a new life in Austria. He loved Ireland and was happy for his sister to have the experience of learning how to navigate the Irish system of schools, housing, etc. As for himself, he enjoyed traveling and Prague was his favorite place so far.

After dinner, we walked over to a tiny, round building in the center of a small park, light blue with white trim. The ornate, lacy trim made it look like a wedding cake. This building housed a small bar that served mostly drinks and pastries. We sat down at one of the six tables and ordered some dessert. The bartender came over when she heard that we were from California she started talking with us. That happened a lot in

Graz. The Austrians welcome every opportunity to practice their English skills. Even when I preferred to speak in German, they could tell I was an English speaker and would keep the conversation going in that direction. There was American music playing in the background, which prompted our conversation to be about its popularity in Europe.

While I was impressed with the bartender's language skills, I was distracted by what was going on behind her. A woman who appeared to be in her late sixties walked in the door wearing a floor-length white dress. Her gray hair was a mess, and her dirty dress dragged on the floor as she took a seat. Looking very content, carrying her disheveled self with grace; she raised her hand in the air and summoned a waitress.

The bartender became aware that something was amiss and went back to work. She spoke discreetly with her coworker while we finished our dessert. Before we paid our bill, we watched as something started up between the lady in white and the bartender: they appeared to be arguing. Soon everyone in the bar took notice. A few minutes passed before our bartender came back to our table. We asked what was happening. "That woman ordered a bottle of our most expensive champagne," she revealed, "and now she does not have any money to pay for it."

The bartender stood at our table, staring across the room at the woman. At that moment, the lady in white stood up and announced to the room, "I am a duchess, and my countrymen shall pay my tab!" To that, the bartender replied sarcastically, "Great."

Shortly after that, the police were called in, and I was surprised at how politely they handled the dispute. The two officers stood beside the woman's table while they allowed her to finish her champagne! When she had, she walked to each table, including ours, bidding us farewell. One officer led her out the door, so I approached the other one and asked, "What will be the consequence of her actions?" The officer replied, "If she is crazy, she will have to pay a fine that reflects her income. If she is drunk, her fine will be higher." It was intriguing to see how respectfully the officers responded to what could have resulted in an ugly scene.

Just another night in wonderland!

JAMMIES AGAIN?

During that same visit with Kevin, Christina and I wanted to take him someplace different and unexpected. We went to a local travel agency and looked through the special offers they had for that month. Istanbul stood out for the same reason Budapest did. It just sounded cool, so we booked it on the spot. The next day we traveled by train to Vienna, where we needed to spend the night before our flight to Turkey the next morning. We strolled the streets of Vienna looking for a place for dinner when we spotted a long line of people waiting to get into one restaurant. There were plenty of other restaurants, but this was the only one with a line. We went to the front of the line to ask why this place was so popular, and the young couple we spoke to said that this was the absolute best place to eat in Vienna and was hard to get into. They don't take reservations, so you just have to wait. At that moment the hostess came over and asked the young couple "How many in your party?" They said "Two," and the hostess said "We only have a table for five available and we won't waste it on a party of two." Instantly we were invited to join them. The five of us sat down with the couple, and it turned out they had a lot in common with my kids. They were in their twenties and the four of them talked about travel, relationships, social media, etc. Katja was from Germany and had a very sweet personality. Her boyfriend was an American marine. The food and friendly conversation was delightful. We were there for two hours, and at the end they exchanged Facebook information and we left for our hotel. Flash forward four years and Kevin and Katja are friends. The met again on Facebook, and they see each other whenever they are in the same city.

The next day, we boarded Turkish Air headed for Istanbul. I was pleasantly surprised to find this small airline to be really quite nice. We sat close to the back of the plane and everyone was handed a menu. The options of appetizers, main course, desserts and drinks were all included in the cost of the flight. Impressive considering these days you could expect to receive a free bag of peanuts on most US flights.

We hailed a taxi to take us to our hotel. The beginning of the drive was uneventful but that eventually changed. As we drove deeper into the compacted city all the automobiles were driving recklessly. At one point, our cab was actually pushing its way through moving traffic. It wasn't much different than bumper cars at a theme park. At one point we were on a rocky hill that had cars fighting to go in opposing directions, horns honking, and no one getting anywhere! Christina said that it reminded her of some harrowing driving experiences she had in India.

When we made it to our hotel, I was disappointed. The area we were in didn't feel safe, and the hotel looked run-down. I decided to at least give it a chance. We checked into our room, where we had three beds and a bathroom, and at least it looked clean. I decided to make the best of it. What the hell? We were in Istanbul! Who cares about the hotel, we were here to discover a cool new city.

Everything we saw outside the hotel was fantastic. Shopping bazaars, mosques, spice markets – I found all of it fascinating to see. I noticed that there were plenty of nice hotels around and wondered why ours was so bad. Still, I tried to not think about it and just planned to spend as little time in our room as possible. What I really enjoyed was how different this city was. Everywhere we looked we were reminded that we were in a land far, far away. The mosques' calls to prayer could be heard coming from many directions. The constant buzz of a foreign language surrounded us as we passed by unique architecture, stone streets, kebab carts, and souvenir stands. The feeling I got from the crowded streets was that everyone was headed somewhere in a hurry. It was the opposite of a city devoted to leisure.

We looked around a bit and found an outdoor café on a random side alley and sat down for dinner. We enjoyed some wine and kebabs before heading back to the hotel. I decided to take a shower, and gathered my toiletries. There wasn't a place for my change of clothes, so I just put them on the floor. While washing my hair, I looked up at the tiny square window above and saw some cockroaches crawling in. I rushed to rinse my hair while dodging the falling bugs. As I got out of the shower, I saw that the bathroom was flooded and my clothes were soaked.

I walked out to our room, and when I saw a bug on the wall above my bed, I lost it. I started tearing up, and Christina tried to make me feel better. Kevin said that he didn't think it was that bad, but it was too late. I was in a rage. Christina went downstairs to the lobby to use the hotel's Internet, and I decided to go downstairs in my jammies with a towel on my head and complain to the front desk. Kevin tried to stop me, saying that I was making a big deal out of nothing. Ignoring him, I ran out of our room and as I was rushing down the iron spiral staircase, I could hear Kevin yelling at me, "Mom! What are you doing? Come back!" I caught a glimpse of Christina sitting in the lobby. She watched my towel-covered tantrum with her face in her hands, shaking her head.

"My room is unacceptable!" I said to the two men behind the desk. "I have stayed in discount hotels before, but this is ridiculous! This was advertised as a middle-class hotel. What is your version of a lower-class hotel? A park bench next to a dumpster?" I then went on to tell them about the bugs and the flooded bathroom. The two Turkish men just stared at me, not saying a word. Finally, when I had finished my rant, they said there was nothing they could do that night, but maybe the next day.

I stomped back up the stairs to our hole-in-the-wall of a lodging, and by then it was almost midnight. I appreciated that my kids were troopers and low-maintenance, but at my age I was less tolerant. I decided we would leave first thing in the morning. We did just that, and found a beautiful five-star hotel. I walked into the fabulous lobby and told the front desk manager how awful our last hotel was. I knew that this hotel was going to be very expensive, and wondered if there was any way we could stay there at an affordable price.

The manager motioned for me to step aside and wait until no one else was around. Then he smiled and slipped me a piece of paper with our special price written on it. It was half the price of their cheapest room, and yet he gave us a wonderful suite! Then he motioned for his associate to bring us each a glass of champagne and escort us up to our room. It was beautiful, and we all were very happy.

I'm sure Kevin and Christina thought I was a little crazy, but you can't blame me for wanting things to be the best that they could be.

The rest of our four-day trip included a boat ride to the Asian side of Turkey, many shopping excursions, an entrance into the Blue Mosque, the spice market and their famous indoor flea market. All in all, everyone had a great time.

SICK

Our visit to Istanbul concluded and we flew together to Vienna. From there Christina flew to Ireland while Kevin and I took the train back to Graz.

Kevin wasn't feeling well on the train, so I was relieved when we found an empty car with lay-flat beds. I heard the train conductor's voice through the speakers and knew in an instant that it was my friend Tony. Tony's German was very recognizable because of his New Jersey accent. When he came by our car, we hugged hello and I introduced him to Kevin. Later that week Tony inquired about Kevin's health since he thought Kevin looked pale when they met.

Waking up the next day in my flat in Graz, Kevin had a high fever and was very weak. He looked terribly pale, and I was worried about him. It filled me with dread, not knowing what was wrong and being sick in a foreign country. I took him to the hospital in a taxi. That was quite an experience. The front desk personnel didn't speak a word of English. My German had been improving, but I didn't have the vocabulary needed to describe Kevin's symptoms. This resulted in my pantomiming diarrhea, fever, and vomiting. The people around me giggled, but understood what I was trying to say. Then I was told in German that I needed to pay one hundred euro up front and that anything left over would be refunded upon discharge.

Only a few minutes passed before we were escorted to a corridor where other patients were waiting. Both sides of the corridor had many doors leading to different exam rooms. People in hospital beds and chairs surrounded us. Each patient was in various stages of care. One guy was in a bed hooked up to an IV, and another was sitting in a chair with a swollen arm due to a bee sting. Some people had already been bandaged but everyone was still waiting for something. Kevin's name was called and we entered one of the exam rooms. I was relieved to hear that the doctors spoke perfect English. A young blond female doctor examined Kevin and concluded that he had extreme food poisoning, most likely from the street food in Istanbul. He was severely dehydrated, so they hooked him up to an IV and rolled him back into the corridor. We waited for two hours while the IV slowly rehydrated Kevin. The young blond doctor checked up on Kevin's progress and ordered another round of fluids.

We spent most of the day there, and I was impressed with the immediate care we received. I was also surprised to find upon leaving the hospital that they refunded us fifty-five euro. Back in the states, a day at the hospital probably would have cost hundreds or even thousands, but in Graz, we were only charged the equivalent of sixty dollars.

KNIGHTS OF THE ROUND TABLE

Not long after my kids' stay in Graz, my friend Vicki from California came to visit me. On one sunlit afternoon, we had lunch at the Glockenspiel, where there is a spacious courtyard surrounded by cafés, shops, and a lot of outdoor seating. Up above is a large clock tower with small doors that open three times a day, revealing a wooden couple, dressed in traditional costumes, who together start the bells ringing. The clock has been operating for over one hundred years. It is a popular place for the few tourists who make their way to Graz. On this day, the weather was exceptional, so everyone was enjoying their lunch under the canopy of umbrellas that shaded the tables.

A mime and a guitar player were entertaining the crowd as we finished our hot dogs and schnitzel. Vicki stopped to photograph the mime when I saw a group of men dressed in regal attire, complete with swords, sashes and feathered hats. They looked like guards for a castle. I walked over and asked them what they were doing. "Come join us!" they said.

As usual, my limited command of the German language and their light grasp of the English language left me unsure of what was about to happen. Before I knew it, approximately twenty of these decorated men formed a line, a parade of sorts, and started marching through the courtyard and up the narrow streets of Graz. I asked one of them, "What do you mean, join you? Where are you going?"

I looked over and saw a surprised look on Vicki's face as she yelled over to me, "What are you doing? Are you in a conga line?" I answered, "They've invited us to join them! Come on!" Vicki ran over and joined me in the parade. She asked, "Where are we going?" I answered, laughing, "I have no idea!"

We marched through the streets of Graz and towards a wonderful ornate church. All along the way, people stopped and stared, snapping pictures of the parade that grew as we went along with the addition of more uniformed participants.

When we reached the steps of the church, there were many people dressed in the same uniforms, while others wore suits and dresses. Unfortunately, Vicki and I were dressed for a very casual lunch. Flip-flops and jeans hardly seemed right for the present circumstance.

Someone in charge gathered everyone together for a group photo on the steps of the church to be taken by a professional photographer. I pulled Vicki to the side so as not to interfere with their photo. Immediately, we were pulled back in, and the group insisted that we be included. I was confused as to what was this was all for, and hid behind the more formally dressed participants. As the photographer took the photos, Vicki stood proudly, a huge smile on her face, and ended up smack in the middle of the picture.

After the photo session, we were invited to join them all in their march to a formal reception held close by. "But we are not appropriately dressed for such an occasion!" I whined. They insisted all the same, so the parade continued up the street to a building at the top of a hill. When we went inside, we were presented with program leaflets and asked if we were ready for what was about to happen. I told them that I had no idea what was about to happen, but also that "If you are inviting us, we accept!"

Inside the main dining room were many long tables with white table-cloths and flowers. They must have been long enough to fit forty people per table. I positioned us at the back of the room in hopes of not being noticed. I would have given anything to have the chance to run home and change my clothes, but I knew that if I did, I would miss everything.

Within minutes, everyone was seated, and at the head of the room was a long decorated table of the sort you would see for a wedding party reception. Everyone seated at that table was in uniform. Next to that same table was a podium with a decorated Austrian gentleman commencing the ceremony. Everything was in German, and the best I could figure was that this ceremony was to honor some of their new members. After the room burst into song, which I believe was their anthem, the doors at the back of the room opened, and two young men carrying large, regal flags led the way for their group of members, who were all clothed alike. This continued with different flags being flown before different groups as they all made their way to the front of the room. Then, speeches were made and many songs were sung.

The people seated next to us spoke some English and were impressed that we were from California. They said that this was a very special event, and it was extremely rare for outsiders to be present. Then, an older, distinguished woman approached our table and was talking to everyone. When she learned that we were from California, she walked over to me and said, "Welcome to Austria! I would like to invite you to a private party to be held in a castle in Graz."

I accepted her invitation with gratitude, and when she walked away, the people seated next to us said, "That woman is a Member of Parliament, and she just gave you an exclusive invitation!" I looked at the invitation and saw that the date of this formal gala was in November. For *this,* I vowed silently, I would be dressed appropriately.

About two hours into the evening, one of the officials from the front of the room made his way to the back where Vicki and I were seated. He extended his hand formally in our direction and asked us to follow him to the front of the room. We were told this evening's man of honor (Vicki and I privately referred to him as "the prince") wanted us to write our names in a huge leather book positioned on its own small table. We did as asked, fully realizing that whatever this book was, it would be a permanent part of their library.

Then, the book was given to the gentleman at the podium. He said a few things in German, and I heard the words "California," and "Diane DeArmond," and "Vicki Snuffin!" We were told that the man we dubbed the prince wanted to meet us. And so, in the front of the room, surrounded by formal apparel, swords, and sashes, Vicki and I were presented to the distinguished gentleman -- in our flip-flops!

He shook our hands, and the event's photographer took pictures as the prince posed with us. Then, we were escorted back to our table, where our new friends exclaimed, "That was quite an honor! You must be excited!" Everything was so over the top and overwhelming, so much so that when we were invited to go to the after-party, I had to decline. We had turned a simple lunch in Graz into an unexpected extravaganza, and I was exhausted.

I never found out what the event was all about, but sometimes I like allowing things to remain a mystery. I was learning to expect the unexpected!

HOSTILE TAKEOVER

During Vicki's visit we decided to take a train from Graz to Budapest. While we were there, we did the usual shopping, castle hopping, dining, and sightseeing. The story I left with comes from the experience we had on the train ride home.

The taxi picked us up from our hotel at two in the afternoon. Outside it was very hot and humid; it felt like it was at least one hundred degrees, and the high humidity made it worse. We walked up the steps of the enormous train station and onto the main platform, where the hardest part of our journey was about to begin. The train station was like an oversized greenhouse that held in all of the heat and humidity like foil around a baked potato. There were people everywhere checking the large electronic schedule board for their departures and arrivals. There were piles of luggage in separate clusters, each being guarded by family members while their designated partners went in search of directions, water, bathrooms, food, or whatever they could find to make this microwave oven more bearable. Most of the men in the building had opted to remove their shirts, and children were sprawled on top of luggage or benches, looking as though they each had a fever and were drifting in and out of consciousness.

Not one person in the building was without something that could serve as a fan -- tickets, maps, or anything they could find.

Vicki and I decided to find our train as soon as possible, claim our seats, and then go look for something cold to drink. Everything was written in Hungarian and I couldn't find anyone who was willing to speak English.

Somehow, in spite of heat and language, we found our train, and it was scheduled to depart in thirty minutes. Perfect! Vicki would guard our seats and luggage, leaving me free to search for something cold to drink. We knew that this particular train did not have a food car, so this was our only chance.

When we opened the door to our train car, the heat almost knocked us off our feet. I don't know how long it had been sitting there, but every window was shut, and without any circulation, the car's interior was worse than the air outside. It was first-come, first-served seating, and the ride ahead was to be over five hours long. "It's okay," Vicki said in accordance with our plan: "I will stay with our luggage on the train and you go find drinks and ice."

I moved as quickly as possible, first waiting in line to buy a room-temperature bottle of white wine, and then in a different line to get two plastic cups, and then another line to talk someone into selling me a bag of precious ice. There was a small counter inside a café where people were ordering food to go. I waited my turn and when the lady running the café asked me what I wanted, I told her that all I needed was a bag of ice. That was obviously the hardest item to negotiate. I could tell that they needed the ice they had to keep their food cold, but after I gave her my best puppy-dog sad face and the rest of my money, she gave in. I was off and running back to the train, through a crowd of miserable people who looked as though they were hallucinating from the heat.

When I opened the door to where I had left Vicki, I couldn't believe my eyes. She was slumped down in her seat, eyes closed, and actually looked as though she had melted. She even appeared smaller than when I had left her just twenty minutes prior. "Oh my God, Vicki! Quick! Get off the train and get some air, I will stay with our stuff." Vicki exited the train and I sat down. As I was sitting in the empty train car, I noticed a man leaning out of the window on the train that was next to ours. What? The windows open? I quickly opened every window in the car, and when Vicki got back on and the other passengers started to board, it was a little cooler. As the train pulled out of the station, a breeze blew through the windows and I thought, "Yes! It can only get better!"

Only five glorious wind-filled minutes had passed when a lady in her late sixties forced her way to my window and slammed it shut. I looked around the car and saw that she had closed every window. What the hell? I jumped up and opened the window. She yelled at me in Hungarian with her arms flying about in anger. I was hot, tired, and thoroughly steamed. "This is my window! I paid for it!" I told her, knowing that she had no idea what I was saying, but I didn't care.

She yelled at me again in Hungarian and threw down my window a second time. My seat was at the front of the train, so I turned around and faced the entire car and yelled, "Does anyone speak English?" I saw five hands go up in the center of the car. "Does anyone speak English and Hungarian?" No takers. Then, I saw someone farther back open her window. I pointed this out to the angry woman and she stormed back to the recently opened window, slamming it shut. This act of hers initiated an argument between the angry woman and five other passengers who spoke Italian.

At this heated moment (no pun intended), the conductor came through our car and was explaining something to everyone, but I couldn't hear or understand him. He made his way to my seat and said that if all of the windows were shut, the car would eventually cool down because there was air conditioning coming through the vents near the windows. I reached over, felt the vent, and it might as well have been three butterflies flapping their sweat-filled wings. "How long will that take?" I asked the conductor. "One hour," he responded. I looked around the car and saw that every window was closed and could tell that everyone was willing to give it a shot, so I closed my window and sat down. Within minutes, the car started to heat up again.

After about ten minutes of me shaking my head in disbelief, a sweet Italian girl who looked to be in her twenties approached me and said with what little English she could command, "We agree with you, but the conductor and some of us in the back are worried about a hostile takeover by the Hungarian woman." I said, "I understand, but you do realize that the light breeze coming through the vents will never cool down this car?" She smiled at me, saying that she agreed, but went back to her seat. I gave the butterflies thirty minutes to cool off the car, and it just got hotter and hotter.

I decided to investigate the rest of the cars on the train and see what they were experiencing. As I walked through crowded car after car, I saw every single window open, curtains flying in the breeze, and felt the cooler temperatures. Every seat was taken. I walked back to my car and stood in the front facing everyone. "This is the hottest car!" I yelled. "Every other car is cooler than this one because *they* have their windows open!" All I got from the passengers were blank stares.

I walked over to my seat and hurled open my window. Instantly, the angry Hungarian charged over, so I positioned myself between her and *my damn window*. She and I stood there, each screaming in our own languages, when surprisingly, one by one, all my fellow passengers opened their windows. The breeze instantly filled the car and started to cool things down. With her face full of rage, the woman went back to her seat. I looked towards the passengers as I turned to take my seat. I was astonished to see everyone on their feet giving me a standing ovation. I looked over at Vicki, who was wide-eyed as she exclaimed, "I have never seen you like this! Wow! Cool!"

For the remaining three hours of the trip, every window was open, except of course for that of the angry Hungarian woman, who remained silent with her window closed. All in all, it was an interesting exercise in crowd dynamics -- what time is the right time to cast off one's long-cherished good manners? That's never easy to say, but there are occasions when you just can't sit still and go along with the program. I had reached the limit of my patience and capacity for discomfort, and found the audacity to do what no doubt many of my fellow passengers wanted to do, but somehow couldn't.

CRITICAL THINKING

Vicki's last night in Graz was spent in one of my favorite places. We were invited to attend a five-year anniversary party for a great restaurant called *Thomawirt*. It had three levels. The first looked like a trendy restaurant/bar, with tables outside and inside and a large bar near a staircase. When you went down those stairs to the lower level, it opened up to another bar, tables, and booths. They had an open kitchen on the left side where you could watch the cooks prepare great Styrian food. The walls were all brick, with lots of arches and curves in the ceiling. On the right side, there were stairs that went even further underground into a bar area where they had local musicians playing live every week. As in the room above, the walls were solid brick, but this room was smaller, almost cave-like, with a large crystal chandelier hanging in the center.

On the night of the anniversary party, there was live music in the streets, waiters dressed in their best uniforms, party trays buzzing by everywhere, and a glass of champagne in every hand. Everything was free! Trays of appetizers, each one better than the one before, were whisked around the outside seating area, and the bar inside was packed with people. The restaurant had at least eight bartenders behind the street-level bar handing out glasses of wine and champagne as fast as they could. The atmosphere was intoxicating, with music and laughter amid the celebrating crowd.

I saw Brendan (one of my new friends in Austria), who had invited us, waving near the staircase beside the bar. "Hey! We have a table downstairs!" Brendan escorted us to the table on the second level he had managed somehow to wrangle. He introduced us to his friends at the table. There was Guillaume from France, a couple visiting from Spain, and Alexander from Russia. They all looked like they were in their late thirties. I was seated across from Vicki, with Brendan on my left and the Russian on my right. We weren't sure how long the complimentary wine would be flowing, so I went upstairs and grabbed four glasses of red wine and brought them to our table. Then Vicki and I went back and forth collecting glasses of wine until the center of our table was filled with approximately twenty-six glasses of wine for our table of seven! Waiters came by with appetizers every few minutes, and the party was in full swing.

The noise level in the room was pretty high, so we all were forced to talk to the person sitting next to us. Vicki was talking to Brendan, so I started talking to the Russian. He opened with, "So, you are from California?" I answered, "Yes." He asked, "Why are you here?" Ask an existential question, get an existential answer: I told him that I had moved to Graz for a new life. He looked puzzled. I asked him, "Don't you like it here?" He responded sternly, "I don't really like anywhere. I think most people are worthless, and it doesn't matter where you live."

I leaned over toward Brendan and whispered, "What's with the Russian?" Brendan said, "Oh, he hates everyone, but we work together, and he's just that way." "Oh . . . okay," I said. I grabbed another glass of wine from our ample supply and drank it down. Then, I looked at my Russian tablemate, who was beginning to seem a bit like some eccentric character in a Dostoyevsky novel, and decided I had nothing to lose. What the hell? I looked him straight in the eye and just started talking, not knowing quite what was going to come out of my mouth.

Well, I told him that every person in the room with us had his own story. "See that guy over there with his wife and kids? He has a story. He might be afraid of losing his job and not being able to support his family. Or maybe one of his relatives that he loves is suffering in the hospital. Maybe tomorrow could be his last day on Earth, and without his knowing it; this could be his last meal with his family. Everyone lives, loves, fears, and hurts the same."

"That is why I joined the bone marrow donor program," I told Alexander. "I think it would be hard to have to go through the pain and needles that are involved with being a donor, but if someone I have never even met needed that from me, how could I refuse? Just say, 'sorry, it would hurt too much to save your life'? You would be surprised how many good people surround you every day, but you just don't know them."

I don't know how long I went on this way, emboldened as I was, but Alexander never said a word. He just stared at me in silence, and when I was finished, he spoke in his heavy Russian accent: "I have never heard such monologue before. I have some thinking to do. I believe I have to change my whole way of thinking." Wow! I looked at him with a huge smile on my face and said, "Really?" He answered, "Yes, really." He looked around the room, and his eyes paused for a moment on the table with the man and his family.

At that moment, Brendan and Vicki brought me into their conversation, and the three of us kept talking. Every once in a while, I would peek over at the Russian, and he was deep in thought while drinking his wine.

I don't know if he ever thought of our conversation again, but I know I did. I was pleasantly surprised to learn that sometimes people really do listen, and maybe, no matter how small the chance, actually change their way of thinking. Who knew that could even happen in these polarized times? It seems my melancholy Russian friend had met his attitudinal match in a California optimist, and the experience was good for us both.

A NIGHT IN VIENNA

I met quite a few people when Vicki and I went to the "Knights of the Round Table" event that I mentioned previously. We exchanged email addresses, and it was such an exceptional evening that I really couldn't remember who was who. A couple of weeks later, someone from that night named Gerard sent me an invitation to join InterNations online. I looked it up, and it was some sort of networking group for global minds and expats. The website had photos of parties and events from all over the world. Everyone appeared to be having a great time. It also stated that the only way to join was to be invited, so I decided to seize the opportunity and join. I received several emails after that, each one announcing different events happening in faraway places, and when they mentioned that an event was going to be held in Vienna, I decided to go.

The next day I bought a train ticket and booked a room at the Intercontinental Hotel. This was where the event was to be held, and I liked the idea of staying on the property. The train ride was two-and-a-half hours of beautiful countryside and little villages. We trekked through stone tunnels and lush mountains sprinkled with churches. Walt Disney himself couldn't have painted a more storybook view.

When I arrived at the hotel, I was happy to see that it was gorgeous inside. I made my way to my pleasant suite and unpacked. I wanted to wear the perfect dress to my first InterNations event. I brought a gray dress that looked like business meets cocktail hour. I had arrived only half an hour before the event, so I quickly changed my clothes and hurried downstairs.

I walked past enormous, elegant chandeliers and dark mahogany walls lined with antique furniture to the beautiful salon where the line already had formed to enter the event. I was a little apprehensive as I stood in line, because I really didn't know what to expect; I just wanted to try something different. I heard other people in the line talking about past events. There was, "Nice to see you again," and a couple of, "This is my first event." I decided to keep to myself until I felt more comfortable.

A woman checking people in handed me my nametag, and I went straight to the glowing bar in the middle of the room. This was where everyone was migrating, and I wanted a seat in a strategic location. As I sat down on the velvet barstool, a couple of men and women my age started talking to me. I told them my brief story of how I ended up in Austria, and they shared their stories in return. One of the women was visiting from Sweden and had been a member of InterNations for over a year. Another said that she lived full-time in Vienna but was originally from Egypt. They were very friendly and made me feel welcome.

The man who had all of the ladies' attention was Stefan. He was a tall Austrian man with movie-star good looks and a personality to match. You could almost see stardust in his eyes. He engaged in conversation with everyone in his proximity, but eventually made his way to me. He sat down at the bar and flashed his perfect smile. I did my best to appear confident, but on the inside I was nervous. Here I was in a new city, with an unfamiliar group of people, and I just didn't want to say anything stupid. Much to my relief, we hit it off instantly! We laughed, took pictures, and scarcely talked to anyone else. I asked him what this event was really for, and he said, "Networking!" I said, "Well, should I let you go network?" and he said with a grin, "I would rather talk to you."

We were only there for an hour when Stefan asked me if I wanted to go for a walk along the Danube River. He was so charming, I said yes. It was a beautiful night. The moon was full and there were fountains, old-fashioned streetlamps, and large trees that filtered the light to make it feel like we were in a painting. We were passing under a large ornamental bridge, and when we were hidden in its shadow, Stefan kissed me. Oh my God! Then, hand in hand, we walked a bit farther to a divine little restaurant on the water with small tables outside. "Would you like to share a bottle of champagne and something to eat?" he asked. "That would be lovely," I replied.

We sat at a candlelit table overlooking what resembled a scene out of a romantic movie set in Paris. We shared champagne, and Stefan fed me small pieces of cheese and fruit. When we were finished, he walked me back to the steps of the hotel. He wanted to escort me to my room, but I thanked him for a perfect evening and let him go.

When I returned to my room, my phone rang, and it was Stefan. He asked me what floor my room was on, and I told him the seventh. He then asked me to look out the window and tell him what the view was outside. "I see a park with large trees," I said. "Look down to the right of those trees, by the streetlamp," he requested. I did, and I saw Stefan waving to me from the moonlit sidewalk below. I waved back, and he walked away.

The next morning, Stefan called and asked if I would join him for lunch before I took the train back. I did, and he spent two hours showing me the beautiful buildings of Parliament, and the many fountains and statues, all the while telling me about their history. We had lunch in an outdoor courtyard with live music playing in the background. I relished the privilege of having a private tour guide.

When he took me to the train, we exchanged email addresses. A quick hug goodbye, and I was on my way back to Graz.

The next day, I emailed him a photo of the two of us from the night before. The only text I added was "So cute!" A few hours later, he sent me a photo of himself lying naked on a beach with the same text: "So cute!" Seriously?

I asked some of my European friends if this was normal, and they said it was not. I came to the conclusion that Stefan was gorgeous, knew it all too well, and therefore wasn't my type. I like men with confidence, not arrogance. A man who is confident doesn't feel the need to prove anything. I thought that sending that photo was his way of saying "Look at me! Aren't I amazing?" Plus, I thought the photo was inappropriate.

The evening we shared was very romantic, and I wouldn't change a thing. I knew I wouldn't see him again, but I was -- and am -- sure there were plenty of women who would.

THIS IS AUSTRIA

The warm weather in Graz was reason enough for Christina to book a flight out of Ireland's cooler temperatures. We had our usual amount of fun-filled days. One afternoon we went to one of my favorite places in Graz for lunch, a restaurant called Purberg. It was a beautiful location that had outdoor and indoor seating. It also had twenty-foot-high ceilings and large glass vases filled with glorious flowers like you would see in a five-star hotel lobby, set on white tablecloths. There was a large bar off to the side that has pastries under glass, and waiters buzzed around with wine glasses filled with berries, champagne, or mimosas. It had such large windows everywhere that the room was flooded with sunlight, making Purberg the perfect place for a Sunday brunch.

Christina and I opted to sit outside on the wooden patio that overlooked a large pond with many ducks gliding across the pristine water. Surrounding the pond was a large forest so green that it rivaled anything I had seen in Ireland. There were a few hammocks hanging in the trees available to anyone interested in swaying in the sun. After our lunch, we took a walk through the forest above the pond and found a small dirt path that led to what I can only describe as a wilderness jungle gym. There in the thick, tall trees were zip lines, rope ladders, and platforms scattered way up high, and the occasional safety nets below. The place was amazing! We saw people wearing helmets and harnesses, and we could hear the clicking of metal clasps as they attached their safety gear from tree to tree.

Christina and I found many trails that led up through the forest, all of them small dirt paths with rocks and tree roots, making it a bit of a challenge to maneuver in sandals. We picked a random trail and headed into the forest. It was strikingly beautiful under the green canopy with the sunlight trickling in through the leaves. We had hiked for about thirty minutes when we found a roughly paved road with wood fences and stone pillars.

As we walked, we heard the faint sound of people talking in the distance. We came upon a large building with a huge rustic gate. Curious about what kind of building would be hidden in the forest, we chose to walk through the gate. We could tell that this was the back entrance. The building was set lower into a hill, and as we walked downward, we could hear people laughing and playing Ping-Pong. "This looks like some sort of recreational center," I said to Christina. "Maybe Kevin can play Ping-Pong here when he comes to visit."

We walked through the back door of the large four-story building and wandered into a lobby. We saw corridors heading in different directions and then three men in white medical scrubs and tennis shoes walking by. In German, I asked one of them, "What is this place?" He pointed to the sign above our heads that said PSYCHIATRIC WARD. We quickly exited the building, feeling rather lucky that they didn't mistake us for patients.

Once we got back on our path, everything looked amazing. We saw open meadows, people hiking or riding bikes, and an older couple sitting at a tiny table in the middle of their garden sipping tea. Most of the walk was slightly uphill, so we started to feel tired and thirsty. Just as luck would have it, we found an incredible restaurant set amidst the trees overlooking the Austrian countryside with the Mariatrost Basilica on the opposite hill. Blue sky and white puffy clouds floated above the vast, tree-framed landscape. This was absolutely gorgeous! This was Austria! This was *The Sound of Music!*

I have never been so impressed by a view as I was at that moment. We stood there in silence taking it all in. The restaurant had its own special appeal. The outdoor seating was on a wood patio that wrapped around the building. Brightly colored umbrellas adorned every table, and flowers overflowed from vases, planters, and hanging baskets. Several levels of seating areas cantilevered over the side of the mountain. We seated ourselves in the middle of it all and watched the waiters walk by carrying trays of large wine glasses filled with strawberries in liquid. In German, I asked the waiter, "What is that strawberry drink?" He answered, "Strawberries in champagne." I promptly said, "We would like two of those, please!"

We relaxed for a while, taking in the magnificent view. Feeling rejuvenated, we headed back down the other side of the mountain. We passed houses with enormous piles of wood stocked up for the winter. Some down hill bikers sped past us and disappeared into the forest. We passed a sign that had the word Graz with a circle around it and a line through it. We figured that meant we were leaving Graz but did not know where we were going. At the bottom of the mountain we found a tram to take us back home.

AMBASSADOR

Fall had officially arrived in Graz, and I was enjoying the fall colors. Not long after I had attended the InterNations event in Vienna, I went to a few of the ones held in Graz. They were a great way to meet new people. One event was a comedy night held in a local bar. A couple events were dinners at different restaurants, and some were cocktail parties. I really had a great time meeting people from around the world.

On one of Christina's visits, we attended an InterNations dinner together. It was still warm in the evening, so we were seated outside at one of Graz's finer restaurants. Settled next to me was the InterNations Ambassador, Marc. He was in his late thirties and had a charismatic personality. Marc and I started talking, and he told me that they needed another ambassador in Graz. InterNations has over three hundred expatriate communities around the world, uniting members of 180 nationalities. Each community has two ambassadors, and Marc's co-ambassador had just resigned.

It was a night of great conversations and laughter. Some of the people new to Graz wanted to know how to navigate the housing system. Starting utilities, registering as a new resident, finding cell service and Internet access are common questions of new arrivals. I observed Marc work the room and noticed that he made sure to acknowledge each and every guest. What I appreciated most was how open and engaged everyone was. I didn't pick up on any hidden agendas, just interested and interesting people sharing an evening. I think Christina had as much fun as I did. At the end of the evening, Marc asked me if I would be interested in becoming an ambassador. I told him that I would love to, but I didn't feel that I had any qualifications or experience. He said that I had great people skills and I would learn the rest along the way. He gave me his number and email and said that he wanted me to think about it.

The title InterNations Ambassador sounded cool! I was a little apprehensive, but I really wanted to give it a try. The next day, with Marc's help, I got in touch with Eva in Germany, who was in charge of appointing people to the ambassadorships. Sitting in front of my computer face to face with Eva was nerve-wracking. I tried my best to show her that I was outgoing and interested in helping manage their Graz chapter. After a one-hour Skype interview, she offered me the unpaid position. The duties for this position were to welcome and seek out new members, organize all the events in Graz, and be available to help expats with any questions they might have.

My favorite part was that I received business cards with my name on them: Diane DeArmond, InterNations Ambassador! This appointment was another experience I would never have predicted before making my way to Austria. It's about serendipity; things just come your way if you're open to the varied experiences that life brings.

The following month, I was to co-host my first event with Marc. We met for coffee and discussed the options for dates and locations. It turned out that this was going to be an anniversary party. InterNations had been around for a long time worldwide, but was fairly new in Graz. Marc said that we should plan on no more than thirty people to attend because our community was still small and growing. I suggested we hold the event in the private dining room at the restaurant in the forest Christina and I had stumbled upon. "Sounds perfect!" exclaimed Marc. "But I need to tell you," he said, "that I won't be able to help you or even attend." "What? Why?" I asked fearfully. Marc explained, "I have personal family obligations that interfere with this month, so I will catch up with you the following month. Don't worry; I will email you all of the member information and what you will need to make up the nametags. Each nametag must include the home-land flag emblem of that member's country. Once you have all of the event information, you must email it to Eva in Germany so she can post it on the InterNations website."

I panicked. I was going to host my first event alone, and it had to be special because it was an anniversary party.

The next day I went to the restaurant in the forest. I spoke with the manager, who showed me their beautiful banquet room. He explained, "We can use white tablecloths and have a single long-stemmed red rose in a vase on every table. I recommend using one of our podiums for greeting guests and a side table to display the nametags." I thought, "Maybe this thing will just plan itself!" He said that there was no charge for the room and they would be happy to offer their full menu. "Done!" After a daylong battle with configuring nametags, formatting the online invitation and sending the necessary information to Eva, I was finished. My first event was to take place in two weeks.

I did not want to host this event alone, so I enlisted my friend Rhys. Rhys and I had been hanging out a lot together, and he had become my "go to guy." Whenever I was looking for something fun to do, I would call Rhys and he always knew what was going on. Whether it was a restaurant opening, art gallery champagne mixer, wine extravaganza, or live music with friends, Rhys was the man to call.

I told him about my upcoming event and he was happy to help. Being originally from England, he spoke English, but it was his grasp of the German language that I thought might be useful. Even though most members spoke English, some of them preferred German. We met at the banquet room one hour prior to the party. I was delighted to find that the room was ready. As the manager had promised, every table had a long-stemmed red rose and the white tablecloths were perfect. A minor dimming of the lights and displaying the nametags was all that was left to do.

As the members trickled in, I received numerous compliments on the venue and was pleased with the turnout. The room was overflowing with banter and merriment. It was electric! After a successful dinner, I concluded the evening with a group photo and everyone had a great time.

I was pleased. I had done something that was out of my wheelhouse and pulled it off. I think there is something to the saying, "fake it till you make it!"

SOMETHING SPONTANEOUS

During his last visit, Kevin had told me about an organization called Couchsurfing. It was an online network of people traveling the world. Anyone could join. Instead of staying in a hotel and occupying your time seeing the typical tourist attractions, you could stay in the home of a fellow couch surfer and learn more about his or her culture and way of life. You don't necessarily stay on a couch. Each member gives a detailed description of the accommodations. Some members can offer you your own guest house, others a private bedroom and bath -- it is all listed on each profile and varies from place to place. I signed up and asked myself, "Where do I want to go?" I had always had Spain high on my list of places to explore, so I searched and found someone named Luisa in Madrid. Luisa was two years older than I was, lived alone, and didn't smoke. She had a private bedroom available, and we would share her bathroom. I read the reviews from other travelers who had stayed with her and they were all positive. I contacted her by email through the Couchsurfing website. The correspondence is monitored for safety purposes and is a good way to figure out your plans before sharing phone numbers, etc. Louisa asked me how many days I was interested in staying, and I said four or five. She said that would be fine and asked when I would like to come. I said, "How about next week?" "That works for me," she responded, and we exchanged phone numbers. It was odd talking with her over the phone because she spoke some English, German, and Spanish. Every sentence was a mix of all three.

I booked my flight the next day, and to save me money on cab fare, Luisa offered to pick me up from the airport in Madrid. I called her cellphone from the curb in front of the airport, and we both laughed when we realized that I was standing right in front of her parked car. She had shyness to her. I wasn't sure if it was because we didn't know each other or if it was our lack of simple conversation. We both struggled with communicating. If only I had paid attention in high school Spanish class, that might have helped. She assisted me with my luggage and then we were off to her place.

It felt crazy to be yet again in a stranger's car in a foreign country, but it was also exhilarating. Here I was soaring through traffic with no idea where we were headed. Louisa was extremely kind and cheerful, so I felt completely safe.

Arriving at her place, she instructed me to "mind the trepps" "Trepps?" I asked. "Yes trepps." She pointed to the steps in front of her door. Inside, she motioned for me to put down my belongings and handed me a key to her front door. Then she gave me a small piece of paper with a hand-written address. Using her English/German, I gathered that this is what she said, "This is your address for the next five days. If you are out and about alone and get lost, just hand this to any taxi driver and he will get you back here. Now let's go, I need to teach you the subway system!" We walked from her place about five minutes to a subway entrance. Louisa was talking the entire time about how she would be at work for a few hours the first couple of days, but would spend as much time as possible showing me the sights of Madrid. Aboard the subway she kept talking about where we were headed, but I had a hard time paying attention. My mind kept wandering to how remarkable this whole experience was, and I had only been there two hours. Suddenly Louisa asked, "So you me tell which now exit we do need?" I didn't know there would be a quiz. She sensed my despair and said that I was sitting on the wrong side of the train. I needed to sit where I could see the station signs as they passed. She also told me that most of the places I would want to go to would be on the blue line. I really didn't have any subway experience, but I would do my best.

We exited the train, walked up the steps, and there we were in the center of the city. I instantly fell in love with the architecture of Madrid. There were typical European buildings with very ornate doors and beautiful moldings. Everything was larger than in Graz. The buildings were bigger, the courtyards were vast, and for some reason the evening sky seemed to reveal more of itself. We sat outside for dinner in the middle of the Plaza Mayor, Madrid's famous central square. Its dimensions are 394 x 295 ft. The sun was setting, and the sky above looked like an oil painting.

After dinner we walked down the many alleys that had plenty of great shops, cafés, bars, and markets, and it was joyously overwhelming! That first evening of my stay was a perfect seventy-five degrees, and the sounds of people, noise, music, and excitement had me awestruck.

Luisa took me to one of the oldest bars in Madrid, and we had an unusual drink. They keep a glass case on top of the bar that is filled with little edible cups. The bartender pulled out two cups and filled them with liquor and handed them to us. The little cup looked like the bottom half of a flat-bottomed ice cream cone the size of a shot glass, and the top half was dipped in chocolate. The liquor tasted sweet, and whatever it was, I liked it! There are Spanish flags flying from some of the buildings that have the symbol of a bear reaching up to the top of a tree. Luisa told me that what we were drinking was made from the fruit of that type of tree.

We spent every day sightseeing, shopping, talking, eating, and walking more than I have ever walked before. It was great, but it also was exhausting. At one point, I realized that although Luisa was a fantastic tour guide, nothing spontaneous was happening. It was day three, and we had been together most of the time. I wanted to go off on my own for just a few hours, and thankfully; Luisa completely understood my need for a little independence.

When I made my request, we were standing in the middle of Plaza Santana, and Luisa decided to go visit her sister, who wasn't feeling well. Meanwhile, I would go explore on my own. Interesting bars and boutiques surrounded us, and it was about 5 p.m. Only two minutes had passed when I walked by a rustic Spanish bar called Corazon Loco. It caught my attention because the sounds pouring out were of people laughing and festive music. It sounded like a party, and the party was right in the doorway and on the front steps of the bar. There was a guy playing guitar and people singing and dancing in the streets. I just had to check this out.

I walked a little closer, and they waved me into their group. A beautiful woman took my arm and said, "If you autograph the tiger's arm, we will give you this hat, and you can drink with us!" I said, "Sure! Where is this tiger you speak of?" She yelled some words in Spanish into the bar, and out came a guy dressed in a tiger costume looking just like Tigger from *Winnie the Pooh!* He rolled up his sleeve, revealing the other autographs he had received that day. They told me that this was a party in celebration of his upcoming wedding. I autographed his arm, and they put a straw fedora hat on my head and sangria in my hand! I couldn't help but smile when the guys introduced themselves: "This is Javier, Jose, Juan, Julio, Manuel, and Miguel" They were all wearing the same kind of hat the woman had given to me.

We drank and danced together, taking pictures of each other and sharing stories. An hour later, they gathered their group, including me, and we walked up the street about ten feet to the next bar. Now the group was smaller, and we were approximately six men and three women. They wanted to know all about Couchsurfing, and one by one they handed me a bar napkin so I could write down the website for them. Even though I had just found out about it myself, I felt like an ambassador for this new way of catching the sights and sounds of the world.

We spent the rest of the night going from bar to bar, and what was great was that they made sure everyone had a glass of water at each stop. No one was drunk, just joyful! At one point, the three women and I broke off from the group to get something to eat. We sat at a small table inside a little restaurant and talked about our lives. Funny to find that even here in this devil-may-care city the women wanted to talk about dieting! We all like to indulge, but we also want to be fit. We also talked about men, clothes, etc. It was a pretty typical drinking conversation between women. They were amazed to hear how I had just picked up and moved to Europe. I don't know how we did it, but by chance, we managed to meet up with the rest of the group at a completely different location.

Shortly after that, I decided it was time for me to go back to Luisa's house, and we said our goodbyes. By the time I got to Luisa's house, it was 1 a.m. and she was on her computer. "How was your night?" she asked. "Great!" I said. I put the hat that I got from the party on the desk and went to bed. So often, the best part of traveling is simply the unscripted nature of it, the way chance seems to take over a traveler's affairs and steps. On this night, I found myself drawn to a place and carried along with a happy crowd celebrating the marriage of a man I had never met. Even though you could say Spain had long been on my bucket list of places to see, this best night of my "couch surfer" visit worked out better -- much better -- than anything I could have planned.

Ultimately, what's the point of traveling? If you want to get the most out of it, you really have to give yourself over, for a time at least, to the life of a strange land, and go where it takes you. The rest of the trip was terrific, too. Louisa took me to meet her mother, father, and little brother in their home. Her father was an artist and took pride in showing me some of his paintings. Her little brother, about fifteen, played soccer and gave me a soccer pin that represented his team. The next day Louisa and I rode bikes to a fountain in a nearby park where we had a picnic lunch with two of her girlfriends.

On my last day Louisa had to work, so I took a taxi to the airport. We have stayed in touch, and I see her occasional travel photos posted on Facebook. What an amazing experience it was! I was lucky to have Louisa be my guide and new friend.

INDIAN NIGHT OUT

In the wake of my Spanish adventure, I would check the Couchsurfing website occasionally for messages or new places to visit. Soon, I received a message from Sunny in India. His message stated that he and two of his friends would be in Graz on business for a few days and were looking for someone to show them around. They already had a hotel, but had never been to Graz before. I thought that being their tour guide for the night would be fun.

I met Sunny and his two friends in the center of the city just before sunset. They were in their late twenties and smiling from ear to ear. They were so excited to meet me and to see Graz! Their excitement was infectious. I first took them to *thomawirt* for a drink, because I like the architecture and the cool vibe it has in the underground bar. I enjoyed seeing the place through their eyes. They really appreciated the unusual cave-like architecture and chandeliers. They wanted to try a typical Austrian drink, so I recommended an Aperol Spritzer. It is three parts Prosecco, two parts Aperol, and one part soda. Next we went to Las Tapas, a Cuban-style bodega with a mix of Spanish and Cuban food and a distinctive atmosphere. It is small inside, and though I haven't been to Cuba, it looks how I imagine a typical

Cuban hangout would look. Dimly lit, rustic iron barstools, cigar boxes, multicolored liquor bottles, candles on tables with hours of candle wax dripping down the sides. Here we sampled an appetizer platter consisting of kebabs, olives, and potatoes.

We stayed at Las Tapas for half an hour before we moved on to Ganesha for an Indian dinner where they met my friend Sathi. It was so entertaining to see my guests laughing and enjoying each place I took them. Sathi joined us at our table and it was great listening to everyone talk about India. It sounds like a place full of colorful people and flavorful foods, and one with a very long, complex history.

After Ganesha, we had time for one more stop, so for contrast I took them to my favorite Irish pub, Original, which I have mentioned in this narrative -- see "One Night in a Bar." My favorite bartender Valentin greeted us at the door, and I introduced everyone. Inside the pub, the crowd was cheery and busily enjoying the many bar games. Sunny and his friends played the plastic crocodile game, and we all took pictures of everything and everyone.

I was pleased that we made it to four different places in one evening and that my guests loved each and every one. Sometimes, as I found in using the Couchsurfing site, you meet people and really nothing much is expected except good company. It isn't a lasting friendship or relationship, but at the same time it's genuine. It's kind of liberating for a change.

CINDERELLA

In my "Knights of the Round Table" entry, I mentioned that I received an invitation to a private gala from a Member of Parliament.

The invitation had a symbol on the front, the date of the event, and the street name without any numbers. It did not list the time or any other details. The date was November 19. Two weeks before the ball, I went online to find the address and was not successful. I went to the Graz Information Center, and they said that this must be a secret society because they didn't know anything about it. I then went to the most popular, elegant restaurant in Graz and showed my invitation to the manager and a couple of local businessmen, and again, they had never heard of it. I then remembered where it all began.

When Vicki and I had noticed the parade of princes, they were emerging from a medieval corridor near the Glockenspiel. I went back to that corridor and saw that the symbol on my invitation and the symbol above the corridor were the same.

I quickly ran up the concrete steps that curved around a stone wall, and I felt like I was climbing a castle. When I got to the top, there was one large door with a doorbell. I rang the bell a few times before someone finally answered. A man wearing a suit greeted me and asked why I had come. I showed him the invitation, and he recognized it right away. "I need more information!" I exclaimed. "What do you need to know?" he asked. I told him that I needed to know what time the event was going to start, and what the expected attire was. "Oh!" he said. "It starts at 7:30 p.m., and I will print out a map for you." He closed the door, and within a couple of minutes, he returned with directions and told me that the men would be in suits and the women would be in cocktail dresses. "Thank you!" I said. "Will you be attending?" I asked. He responded, "Yes, of course!"

The night of the ball I wore a beautiful black dress and new shoes. I had on my only diamond necklace and sheer black stockings. It was very cold outside, so I had my long black coat and gloves.

I hailed a cab and gave the driver my map. He spoke German and a little English. "Ok, I know this place." he said. We were on our way, and I was so excited! After a twenty-minute drive, we pulled up to a large building that was completely dark and empty. There wasn't even one car in the parking lot. "Are you sure you have the right night?" he asked. "Yes!" I said. I showed him my invitation. He looked at it and then made a few phone calls. Each person he called said that they had never heard of this secret society. The map said that the address was 3 Meerscheinschlössl, and that was where we were. We drove around for a while checking nearby locations, and after thirty minutes I had to give up. I was so disappointed.

All dressed up with no place to go, I opted for one of the many nice restaurants in Schloßplatz. There was a splendid cobblestone pedestrian area with narrow alleys, gold lighting, and little shops. The cabbie dropped me off as close as he could which was at the top of a small hill. I had to walk the rest of the way. As soon as he drove away, I realized that I had left my gloves in the cab.

With freezing hands, I went inside one of the more upscale establishments and sat at a table in the bar. I was feeling disheartened and alone with my glass of wine when a young couple sat down next to me. "How are you this evening?" they asked. "Well," I said, handing them my invitation, "I am supposed to be at this!" The young man looked at it and said that he would try to help. He made some calls and used his phone to go online, and said, "Ah! You need number thirty, not number three." "Are you sure?" I asked. "Yes, definitely number thirty." I thanked him, paid my tab, and was off to give it one more try.

As I walked up the hill towards the spot where the cab had dropped me off, I noticed a large group of very nicely dressed men my age headed in the same direction. When we reached the top, they stopped me and asked where I was going. I told them that I was going to a party. One of the men reached out his hand and asked, "Is this your glove?" "Yes!" I said, "but I had two!" He then he looked around and magically produced my second glove.

I was surprised to see that even though it was a damp night, both gloves were clean and dry. I thanked him and he said, "This is my sixtieth birthday, and if for any reason you leave your party, we would love for you to join ours!" He then pointed out the restaurant they were headed to. I said, "Thank you, and happy birthday!"

I walked a little farther and found a cab. "30 Meerscheinschlössl please!" The driver responded, "I don't believe that there is a number thirty." I asked him to try anyway, and off we went. On Meerscheinschlössl, the driver pointed out that the highest number on Meerscheinschlössl was sixteen. I couldn't believe how challenging this was. I even wondered if that was part of the secret evening. Finding the venue was your rite of passage? Disappointed again, I asked him to take me back to where he had picked me up.

Since I failed to find the ball, I would attend a stranger's birthday party. I walked down the hill to the restaurant where the birthday party was. Sounds of laughter and clinking glasses filled the entryway of the gorgeous Austrian bistro. I walked inside and found that they had a private room with one large table in the center and an empty chair for me. When the men noticed that I had come, they all stood smiling and applauding, welcoming me to their dinner. How great was that? I was the only female in a room full of happy, successful gentlemen. I quickly learned that they were all doctors. They were so sweet, and each one wanted to have their picture taken with me. "You look like a movie star!" one of them said. I felt like Cinderella at my own private ball!

I was seated next to the birthday boy, Christoph. Christoph had an endearing smile and it was apparent that his friends cherished him. One by one they each stood and said nice things about him in English. I engaged in small talk with everyone throughout the evening. By the end Christoph and I hit it off so we exchanged phone numbers.

You're probably wondering what the deal was about that secret society. Well, I never did find out. But you know what? It didn't matter one bit that my primary invitation had turned into a pumpkin. There are times when you really must tie up loose ends, and there are times when, seemingly of their own accord, they make such a wonderful arabesque that nobody would wish things had turned out otherwise.

MARBLE FLOORS

It was almost New Year's Eve. In Austria and other European countries, they call this night "Silvester," the Feast of Pope Sylvester I. It celebrates December 31 much as we do in the States with parties and late-night fireworks.

I didn't have any plans for Silvester until I received a phone call from Christoph. I had talked to him a couple of times on the phone, but I left for the US shortly after his birthday party, so we hadn't met again in person.

As usual, Christoph was very pleasant to talk to, and during our conversation, he insisted that I join him for dinner and dancing to bring in the New Year. He gave me his address and I took a taxi to his place. The plan was to start the evening with a glass of champagne before heading out to a nice restaurant for dinner. He greeted me with a smile and a hug and was excited to give me a tour of his penthouse. "Let me start with the garage," he said while guiding me with his hand on my back. "This is my Mercedes and the empty space next to mine could be for your car," he said with a wink. That's odd, I thought to myself. Then we went upstairs where he showed me his new marble floors, his porcelain vase collection, office, remodeled kitchen and art collection. "My marble floors are heated!" he proclaimed proudly. Then he pointed to a large oil painting hanging above the couch. It was a field of flowers and obviously very old and expensive. "This could be left to your children someday." I just smiled and said, "It's lovely." What was he talking about? I thought to myself. We made our way to the master bedroom closet where he had his clothes nicely displayed and pointed out that half of the closet was empty. "Plenty of room for your clothes if things go well!"

This was strange. We barely knew each other, and Christoph was already planning for me to move in. We sat down in the living room and he poured our glasses of champagne. I took a healthy sip and toasted our evening. He turned up the festive music on his impressive sound system and handed me a small wrapped gift: "This is a tradition in Austria; open it." I opened the box and inside was a beautiful sterling silver four-leaf clover. "It's very nice," I said. "Thank you." He explained that the clover was to bring good luck in the New Year, and then he handed me a small ceramic pig and said that it, too, was for luck.

We finished our champagne and drove to Café Sacher in his shiny new Mercedes. I had been there for lunch, but it was all dressed up for Silvester. The two of us enjoyed dinner, listened to lively music outside and went for a walk in Hauptplatz where the fireworks were sounding off. It was a long evening. I took a taxi home and went to bed exhausted.

Christoph called at 7 a.m. the next morning. "Join me for coffee -- I'm down the street from your flat." I had only gotten five hours sleep and had a headache. "Thank you for the invite but I'm not up for coffee right now." This really irritated Christoph. "I am not asking for too much, just that you join me for coffee." I replied, "I am still in bed and we had a late night, so how about some other time?" Again, he sounded angry. "I don't think you are being fair. Its just coffee." I said that I didn't want to argue about it, I just wasn't up for going anywhere. We ended the conversation and I went back to sleep.

The next night I joined Christoph for a glass of wine at a local pub. He seemed different, as if he had something on his mind. He asked me to come to his home for dinner, but it felt like he was testing me. I said that I already had plans for that night. "Fine, I will invite a flight attendant who is a friend of mine. She is very beautiful." He waited for my reaction. "Okay" was my response. I could see the fire in his eyes. He wanted me to be jealous, and I was already over this guy.

Two days later, Christoph called again, and this is how the conversation went -- no exaggeration:

"I made up the story about the flight attendant."

"So you lied!"

"No, this is not lying, I just wanted to see how you would react."

"That is lying!"

"No it isn't."

Then, before I knew it, I found myself in a heated argument with someone I hadn't spent enough time with to care about. I very rarely argue. It's just not the way I relate to people. I tried to end the conversation with, "I don't want to fight with you, Christoph, I will talk to you later." He kept on yelling at me and wouldn't let me get a word in. Finally, I hung up on him, and picked up again only because he promptly called back over and over:

"How dare you hang up on me! Here in Austria we have better manners than you Americans. We would never hang up on anyone. Who do you think you are hanging up on me?"

"I tried to end our phone call, but you wouldn't stop talking. I don't want to see you anymore and I certainly don't want to argue with you."

He kept yelling at me about breaking up with him and hanging up on him, and my being a rude American. I raised my voice to get a word in, "Okay then, we have nothing left to say, so let's hang up now." Still he kept on yelling. I tried again. He wouldn't stop. I said over and over that I wanted to hang up, but he wouldn't shut up. Finally, I yelled into the phone, "THAT IS WHY I HUNG UP ON YOU! YOU WONT LET THE CONVERSATION END! I'm hanging up now Christoph, goodbye."

And I hung up on him.

I still hadn't had enough experience with Austrian men to conclude that this was typical behavior. I would prefer to believe that this was not the common way new relationships start.

CROATIA

Winter and spring passed uneventfully. I spent most of the time running errands and keeping warm. The snow was beautiful; just enough to look like a Christmas card. Summer was in full swing when my daughter Christina arrived on a Wednesday for a weeklong visit. I thought it would be great to take her to Croatia. I wanted to see it again, and Christina had never been. I went to the local travel office and found out that the only train or bus that went to Croatia from Graz ran Saturday to Saturday, and we didn't want to be gone for a whole week. The only other option was to rent a car and drive there. Since Christina couldn't find her driver's license, I would have to be the driver. To make matters worse, it was going to be expensive to take the car through Austria, Slovenia, and Croatia with full insurance. The only automatic-transmission vehicle available was a large Mercedes for an additional two hundred euro, so I opted for the car that had a stick shift to save money. I hadn't driven stick for at least thirty years, and knew that I would have to relearn it in the parking lot when we picked up the car.

On the morning of our trip, we went to the rental office located at the Graz airport and had them add a navigation device because all of the MapQuest directions we could find were in German, and I knew that would be too difficult. We got into the car, which was parked in an underground garage with concrete pillars and tight turns. I was really rattled, because I didn't get to practice. We were off and running through complex airport turnstiles and one-way streets, then accelerating onto the freeway. Christina was helpful with the calming words, "You are doing great, just keep going!"

After half an hour, I loosened my grip on the steering wheel and tried to relax. There are a lot of mountains between Austria and Croatia, so they made the roads easier to travel by tunneling through them. We counted, as we passed through twenty-three tunnels. Some of them were so long and dark that it looked like the middle of the night even though it was mid-day.

We were two hours into our trip when dark clouds hovered above the mountains. I thought of how the people in Southern California over-react to the slightest bit of rain on the highway. Just as we were crossing a large bridge high above a deep crevasse between the mountains, the sky suddenly opened up and pounded down the heaviest rainfall Christina and I had ever witnessed.

It looked like milk because everything went white, and we had no idea how to turn on the windshield wipers. The sound of the rain on the car's roof was deafening. I started to panic. Christina was trying to find the button for the wipers, and I couldn't see the road at all. I slowed almost to a stop, while Christina and I yelled at each other to be heard over the sound of the rain. Christina screamed, "Keep going! We are going to be hit from behind if you don't!" I yelled back, "I can't see anything, and I don't want to drive off the side of the bridge or hit a car up ahead." There was no space to pull over, and I was driving blind.

I don't know how long the nightmare lasted, but it felt like forever. Christina figured out the wipers and we made it to the other side. As quickly as it appeared, the rain was over, and shortly after there were clear skies and sunlight. I was frightened almost out of my wits for the next hour or so, feeling afraid of every cloud in the sky, but soon I got over it.

We drove to the Island of Krk. Krk was one of the largest Adriatic islands, and it had a rich history with Roman and Italian influences. I chose Krk because I had been there before with Hans so it would be familiar to navigate. We checked into our hotel and went exploring. It really was beautiful. The water was crystal clear in every shade of blue, and the temperature was perfect twenty-four hours a day. There were so many little cafés and incredible places to see! We did our best to take it all in.

One evening, as we were enjoying a lovely dinner outside next to a castle, we heard the couple behind us talking. They started singing happy birthday in German, so Christina and I raised our glasses in their direction toasting their celebration. They were thrilled with our participation and insisted that we join them at their table.

They looked my age and they were both Austrian. They told us their names, but because we couldn't pronounce them, I never committed them to memory. We talked for a while, and then when it started to rain, we moved to a covered portion of the restaurant. The rain was really coming down, and it was great to watch it from our cozy little table. We celebrated together for about an hour before Christina and I asked for our check. The birthday boy said, "Absolutely not! This is my party and I insist on picking up the tab!" "Thank you so much, but you really don't have to," we explained. "I insist!" he said. "And we would like to meet you both here tomorrow night at eight, and you can buy a round of drinks then." We agreed and said goodnight.

The next morning, Christina and I drove to the medieval town of Vrbnik and passed through a small vineyard on the way. We talked to a waiter in the village, who explained that the vineyard belonged to the Cardinal, and they only sold that wine in one location in Vrbnik. We quickly found the right place and sampled the wine. It was such a special and rare find that we told them we would like to buy a mixed case of the Cardinal's wine, if that was alright.

The agreeable waiter escorted us upstairs where the wine was kept. On a small table at the top of the stairs, Christina noticed a ball-shaped bottle the size of a tennis ball that had a pewter label mounted on the side. "That is the champagne." The waiter told us. "How much is it?" I asked. "Eighty-eight Kuna," he replied, which was about twelve euro. "I want everything!" I said jokingly. We put together a box with five bottles of red wine, five bottles of white, two bottles of dessert wine, and five of the small round bottles of champagne. He threw in a sixth free of charge. After we paid for our wine the waiter walked us to our car.

"We raided the Cardinal's wine cellar!" Christina and I giggled all the way to the car, where were shocked to find a ticket on our window, a sticker that sealed the driver's side window to the frame of the car, and a big yellow iron boot mounted to the front tire! Apparently, we had parked in a space that required a parking pass, but nothing was in English, so we didn't know.

I was trying to unlock the trunk so the waiter could put down the case of wine, when the parking officer who had put our vehicle in shackles approached us. I don't know what was said between the officer and the waiter, but I could tell that the waiter was pleading our case and the officer was reluctant. After hearing the words "American," "California," and something about our ignorance, the officer agreed to let us go with a fine of one hundred Kuna (about 13.50 euro), payable on the spot. We paid the fine, hugged the waiter, and went on our way.

Back at the hotel, we got ready for our cocktail hour with the couple we had agreed to meet at eight. It was another superb evening, and we admired the blue ocean water as we walked along the boardwalk. Before we reached the restaurant we had been to the night before, we spotted our drinking buddies at a table outside near the water. They were approximately five minutes from our designated meeting place.

They waved us over, and we sat down together ordering a glass of wine. Only a few minutes had passed when our waiter from the night before and another gentleman approached our table. "Hello!" we said, happy to see them. Then we noticed that they weren't smiling. "You left without paying your bill last night," they said sternly. Christina and I looked at each other and had no idea what they were talking about. We explained that the gentleman we were seated with then and now had offered to pay the bill, and we believed that it was all taken care of. However, at that moment the birthday boy had very little to say. Again the waiter accused us of skipping out on our tab. Still silent, the birthday boy shrugged his shoulders. Finally, the waiter started questioning him and the conversation was in Croatian. Needless to say we didn't know what was being said, but it ended with all eyes on me. This was crazy! Why did he offer to pay and then leave us to take the blame for skipping out on the check? I never did get an explanation.

Confused, we offered them a credit card, and they said that they would only accept cash. We didn't have any cash, and when we offered to go get some, they said that only one of us could go and the other would have to stay. Christina offered to go because she would rather go to the bank than stay with this senseless bunch. The manager escorted Christina to the nearest bank, where she withdrew the money and paid the bill. When she returned, she said, "Well, that was a terrible walk of shame!" She said that during the walk the manager made comments to shop owners along the way in German, and whatever he said prompted dirty looks towards Christina.

I felt angry that they made us feel like criminals, so we went back to the restaurant where we had been the night before. I talked to the manager and the waiter, explaining that we were good people who would *never* walk out on a bill and that this was a terrible misunderstanding. They softened up a bit, and we left things on a lighter note.

The following night in Krk, Christina and I had dinner at an Italian restaurant with large wooden picnic tables. The owner asked us if we wanted to try the fish that he had caught that day, but we opted for the pizza instead. He brought over a small plate with anchovies and sardines in oil. It looked like something neither of us would enjoy, but not wanting to offend him, I wrapped it up in my napkin when he wasn't looking. When the coast was clear, Christina took the fish down an alley to some local kittens that were very excited to eat them for us.

It was about eleven o'clock when the restaurant started their closing process, and a nice guy named Peter joined our table. He said that he was originally from Krk but was currently living in London. He and Evan, the restaurant owner, were great friends, and after the restaurant was closed, the four of us drank wine that was made by the owner's family.

We took a walk together along a stone street that I had been down at least five times already, but this time we passed through a wooden doorway that I had never noticed before. It was *amazing!* The building had recently been sold. The new owner wanted to know what was underneath and had started digging. What he found were the remains of walls and large stone baths that were built when the island was under Roman control . . . around 50 BCE! That would have been the late Republican Era -- just around the time Julius Caesar crossed the Rubicon River.

Well, the owner had since incorporated the old construction with the new to create a unique setting for a bar. The first floor had tables with a large, impressive wooden bar and there were lots of small sitting areas and nooks in which to relax. The lower level had all of the ruins and lanterns to light the way through large hallways. I guess the whole setup was what you might call "repurposing" an exciting period in history. It's hard to think of a more fertile place to do that than parts of old Europe. To be an American in such places is to feel like a child. Up the stairs and outside in the back of the building were lots of trees, benches, fire pits, bars, and a fantastic laser light show shining down on the sand below patrons' feet. We had a great evening.

Christina and I spent the next day traveling from village to village, taking pictures and enjoying the sun. We spent a total of four days in Croatia, and on the last evening, we heard a young couple speaking English. We talked to them for a little while, and they told us that they were from Boston and they had never been to Croatia before. We agreed to show them a really cool place up the street when they finished their dinner. We showed them that incredible "Roman" bar and they were blown away! So we had gone from newcomers to would-be tour guides in less than a week -- not bad!

We left the couple at the bar and were heading back to our hotel when we passed the restaurant where we had that embarrassing payment problem. We sat down to order a snack, and soon the manager came over with two glasses of wine for us. He said with a smile, "Compliments of the restaurant! To bury the hatchet!" We all laughed and were happy to put the misunderstanding behind us.

BUDAPEST

Our stay in Croatia had come to an end. Christina and I left our hotel at two o'clock in the afternoon. We were about forty-five minutes from Austria when we noticed signs for Budapest. Christina looked it up on our navigation device and saw that it would take three hours to get there. "Wow! That would be cool! Just the name BUDAPEST sounds like an adventure!" she cheered. I got caught up in the idea and asked if there were any reasons why we shouldn't extend our trip another day. We couldn't come up with any, so we took the next exit and off to Budapest we went.

We were driving through Slovenia and didn't see any signs or borders when we crossed into Hungary. We needed to stop for gas, but we were in the middle of nowhere. We finally found a large gas station on the side of the road, and a man quickly offered to pump our gas. We didn't speak the same language, so it was hard to explain to him that I could pump it myself. That apparently was not an option. He took the gas hose from my hand and started filling my tank. After he was finished, he said "fifteen thousand."

"Fifteen thousand what?" I asked. He pointed towards the building that was filled with snacks and booze. We walked in, and since we both needed to use the restroom, we got in line. There were about six women in front of us, all dressed differently. Most of them had scarves around their heads. There was a man mopping the floor and a lot of water on the ground. I could tell that there was a problem, but couldn't figure out what anyone was saying. I leaned in and looked around the corner and saw that the plumbing had overflowed and flooded the floor.

Before I could share that information with Christina, she said, "Geez! I don't think they need to add any more water; it's wet enough!" She thought the man with the mop was wetting the floor to clean it. We both laughed when I told her that they weren't adding, but getting rid of the water.

We skipped the restroom and went to pay. "Fifteen thousand," said the man behind the register. "What is the currency here?" I asked. "Foreign," he said. "I know it's foreign," I said. "But what is it?" "Foreign!" he replied. Hmmm . . . . I handed him my credit card and it went through. It turns out that the currency there is called the *forint*, but it sounded like he was saying foreign. Basically, we were having a "Who's On First?" conversation straight out of Abbott and Costello.

We drove for a couple of hours, and the landscape wasn't looking any different. "I hope Budapest looks different from Austria and Slovenia, or it might not be worth the trip!" I said. "Oh no, I've seen photos on the Internet -- it looks really cool," answered Christina. We kept driving, and when I saw a large black storm cloud ahead, I got nervous. "It will be fine," Christina said to make me relax, but I didn't want to relive that last rain experience we had in Croatia.

We were just about twenty miles away from Budapest, and it still didn't look like much. "It's okay, we will make the best of it," we agreed. Finally, up ahead, it started to look more like a city. Then, the road narrowed, carrying us towards a mountain and down through a dark tunnel, and what I saw on the other side blew my mind! Suddenly, we were crossing an enormous, enchanting bridge that was suspended over a river, and we were headed towards large Gothic buildings and statues of lions. It was difficult to drive because the sights were so amazing. Cars were quickly driving past us, and I tried to stay out of everyone's way. I parked on a side street. "This is amazing!" was all Christina and I could say.

Using her cell phone, Christina looked up hotels in the immediate area: "The InterContinental looks beautiful and has a view of the river and the famous Chain Bridge." We parked the car near the main entrance. Christina waited in the car while I went in to book us a room. Since we had just left a beach city, I was wearing shorts, a T-shirt and flip-flops. My hair was a mess, and overall I looked like I couldn't afford the InterContinental. The people coming and going inside the hotel lobby were impeccably dressed. In fact they looked wealthy and polished, so much so that I felt embarrassed as I approached the front desk. "I would like a room for the night, please." As I spoke, the two women behind the desk gave me an inspective once-over, rolled their eyes, and said "The hotel is totally booked for tonight. Perhaps you could find something a few blocks over." I didn't know if that was true or if they didn't think I was good enough for their hotel. Feeling disconcerted, I went back to the car. Christina did a bit more research again on her phone and found a decent Radisson Hotel a few blocks away. We booked a room, dropped off our luggage, and went to roam the streets in search of a great place for dinner. We ended up at a really incredible spot. There were several restaurants all in a row with outdoor tables and gorgeous lights and candles everywhere. Each one was adding its own unique music to the atmosphere. We picked a spot with a quaint table outside in the middle of all the lights. After dinner, we walked around just looking at the beautiful architecture trying to take it all in.

In the morning, we wanted to take on the day, so right after breakfast, we checked out of the hotel and went sightseeing. Large trees, Gothic churches, bridges, and cathedrals surrounded us. We walked across the same bridge that we had driven over the night before. We learned that it was the famous Chain Bridge, which had been built in the mid-nineteenth century and then rebuilt after World War II. We walked up the meandering path through trees and archways to the Buda Castle on the hill overlooking the river where we had lunch.

After lunch, we walked to a local shopping area where we found lots of excellent shops and things to see. We wanted to find something off the beaten path, like an antique store down an alley. We picked a direction at random and started walking. After a few blocks, we happened upon exactly what we were looking for: an antique store with lots of character. Inside, the shelves and floors were crowded with unusual collectables. There were a lot of ornately decorated old furniture pieces and cases filled with estate jewelry. A narrow, steep staircase led to a second floor packed with so much furniture and paintings that it was difficult to navigate through. Downstairs, Christina was having a conversation with two elderly Hungarian women who ran the store. Their eyes lit up as they shared the history behind each trinket Christina pointed to. Then Christina's eyes locked onto a small jewelry box in a glass cabinet. "What is the story behind this?" she inquired. They told her that the blue glass used to make the box was common for Hungarian aristocrats to have in their possession and that it was hand-painted in Hungary before WWII. "Sold!" Christina and I left with her newfound treasure.

The drive back was blissfully uneventful. No heavy rains, and I was finally comfortable driving through foreign countries in a stick-shift car.

The trip to Budapest was superb, and neither one of us ever will forget it. Once again, we had found that sometimes the best kind of trip is the one you didn't plan.

A SPECIAL DAY

After a few years of living in Graz, when I met new people they would ask me if I lived there alone, and I would say, "Yes, but I am not really alone -- I am dating Graz! I love this city!"

During one of Christina's visits, we looked inside an antique jewelry store. The charming gentleman behind the counter was obviously in a relationship with each glorious piece of jewelry, because he knew every detail and the history behind each one. We really liked the tiny antique boxes that accompanied the special items.

It was December, and I walked the streets of Graz running my errands. I saw the shop owners decorating their stores for the holidays. There were forklifts raising men in the air to assemble the many light displays. Down every street there were decorations, lights being hung, and miniature Christmas trees hanging above. The skies were dark gray, so every light was on. People were dressed in beautiful coats, scarves, and boots. The children were bundled up in knit hats and gloves and looked like they had been pulled from a Norman Rockwell painting, Austrian style. It really was a beautiful sight, Graz in Christmastime.

On my way back home, I passed another jewelry store that was on my street. I saw an antique ring in the window in one of those wonderful antique boxes. I went inside and tried it on. It was perfect! The jeweler told me that this ring was from the Austro-Hungarian Empire and that it had been made during the mid-nineteenth century.

I decided to make my relationship with Graz official. As I purchased that history-steeped old ring, I thought about all the special memories the city and I had made together and about my hopes for more in the future. I thought then and still think now, "I know that wherever life takes me, my heart will belong to Graz."

AUF WIEDERSEHEN

In mid-December, I had to leave Austria. I had stayed longer than I was allowed to without a visa. I would try to return on December 30, but there was a chance that I would be stopped at passport control at the airport. Even though I had stayed too long, it was difficult to see what was what because I had so many stamps on my passport that even I couldn't tell how long I had been in the European Union. My passport at that time did not have a microchip, but my next one would. The microchips make it easy to track one's travel. If I were allowed back into Austria, I planned to have my papers in order to apply for a visa on January 2.

Two days before my flight back to the U.S., I couldn't help but see Graz through the eyes of someone who might not be allowed to return. I took my camera with me on my last night and snapped photos of the things I would miss the most if I were not permitted to return.

I boarded the tram that I had traveled on too many times to count, and saw the people smiling and sharing their day in a language that I had grown to love.

I walked by the man selling pretzels on the corner, whom I had seen every day since I moved to Graz. He always looked happy in his white chef's coat. I took photos of my bank, my street, my phone store, and the tram itself. I took photos of the tram signs that changed as each destination passed, and of my favorite storefronts. It wasn't until I saw the enormous Christmas tree in the center of Graz that I started to tear up. I asked a local merchant when the tree lights would be turned on and he said December 21, the same day that I would be on a plane to the USA.

I hid my tears and walked over to a little stand that was selling *Glühwein*, a local holiday wine that is served hot and tastes like Christmas. I took photos of the many *Maroni* stands that sold hot roasted chestnuts wrapped in newspaper.

The sun was setting, so the lights turned on one by one, lighting up the chilly winter city like a Christmas card. I saw the clock tower and the ornate buildings in Graz, and I found myself missing a place that I hadn't even left yet. An odd sensation, you may say, but as I think back on it, it holds up well. We really can "miss" a place whose streets we still traverse. Maybe that's because our sense of place is so bound up with belonging, with routine even in variety, and a feeling of permanence even in the flux of travel.

I walked into a little pub and sat down at the bar. Seated next to me were the owner of the pub and a female friend of his. "Why do you want to stay in Graz?" they asked. I stumbled over my words, trying to explain to them in German how special I thought Graz was. "Ich liebe es hier. Die Menschen, die Architektur, denke ich, Graz ist sehr süß!" (I love it here. The people, the architecture . . . I find Graz very sweet!) In that way, I expressed my love for the city and its people. Then I took out my camera. I turned on the display to show them the recent photos I had taken of Graz that night.

They accepted my camera, and together they examined each and every picture, smiling and pointing out everything they recognized. "Oh! The tram!" The woman smiled. "I have never seen it look so beautiful!" They talked to me for a little while, and when we were finished, the owner said in his broken English, "This is special thing you did. You give up all to be in Graz. I see you love here. I hope you get visa. I hope you stay." I took a picture of the couple and we hugged goodbye. I found it endearing that their own city looked even more striking to them through a stranger's eyes.

GAME OVER?

I spent the holidays in the States visiting family and friends. Flying back to Austria afterwards was nerve-racking. I had a stop in Frankfurt, Germany, and my hands were shaking as I passed through passport control. I watched the few open stations to see if any officer looked easier to get past than another. One line looked like it was moving faster so I figure that officer might not be taking time to really review each passport. I changed over to that line and waited for my turn. The officer looked at my passport and asked me how many days I had been in the European Union over the past twelve months. Without a visa, non-residents only are allowed to be in Europe for six months out of twelve. I had been there well over that. I looked him straight in the eye and lied, "three-and-a-half months." As he flipped through my passport pages I thought a distraction might interrupt his train of thought so I said "Oh how cute! Look at that puppy wearing a sweater!" He took his eyes off my passport and looked in the direction where I was pointing." Oh, you just missed him" I said with a smile. He then stamped my passport and waived me through. I was so relieved when I landed in Graz; their passport control was closed, so I was home free!

I had spent many hours gathering information on obtaining a visa. I found that every website gave a different answer than the one before. I quickly learned that the most effective way was to do everything in person. Even when the government employees I spoke with understood English, there was always a translation problem.

I was told that I had a lot of paperwork to gather and that special stamps were required. During one of my office visits, I was told that it was mandatory that I have an Apostille stamp on my "proof I am not a criminal" document. One month later, I was told that the $150.00 Apostille stamp was only required on my birth certificate, and that the birth certificate needed to be less than three years old. Mine was older so I ordered a new birth certificate, and then mailed it to the USA Government office for the Apostille stamp.

During my following visit to the visa office in Graz, I thought I had everything they had requested: proof of all my banking accounts, monthly bills in Austria, Austrian health insurance, non-criminal record, a document from the Austrian Police Department stating that I was registered in their country, proof of divorce, etc. They examined my paperwork and said that I needed to return to their office on the first Monday in January. I had heard conflicting information on how many visas are awarded per year, but now I know that they only allow thirty per year, and they are all gone by the end of January.

I wanted to be the first in line at the visa office on January 2. I arrived at 4 a.m. in the dark, cold, empty corridor of the visa entrance. I was the second person to arrive, and the line slowly grew before the office opened at 8 a.m.

When my number was called, I rushed to my appointed room, Number 203. The woman behind the desk looked over my paperwork and said that a new requirement had been issued. Now, I needed to be enrolled in German 1A and she gave me a list of qualified schools. If I had known this, I would have started the class a long time ago. She also said that I needed documentation to prove that I had passed the final exam.

I signed up for the necessary class and returned to the visa office with my class application and receipt. Then they said they wanted two more passport photos. I found the nearest passport photo place, which happened to be an electronics store. I submitted those to the visa office and was finished for the day.

On February 16, I was called back to the visa office. Apparently, they needed the German 1A exam diploma by February 29. I tried to sign up for the exam and found that it was government-controlled. They required registration for the test to be submitted six weeks prior to taking the exam. This, I knew at once, was an insurmountable bureaucratic obstacle: game over.

My new plan was to finish my German classes, pass the exam, and resubmit my application next January. I also considered moving to Prague, because there they issue two hundred visas per *day!* Can you believe that?

Anything worth having is worth fighting for, and now I was faced with another year of living in and occasionally leaving the European Union.

SNOW

It was a very cold winter day in February when Rhys called to say hello. There wasn't any snow yet, but it looked like there might be some on the way. He started talking about how much he missed his TV entertainment, and I offered to bring my Popcorn Hour over for him to borrow. It was a device that held hundreds of movies.

Rhys lived in his family home, which he had inherited when his grandmother died years ago. His grandmother and his mother grew up there, and it was a typical old Austrian home. The outside was painted yellow with brown trim. The ceilings were low and made up of many dormer windows, vaults, and beams. A steep, narrow staircase led to the kitchen upstairs. It was small and had a wooden table with two chairs near a door that opened up to a rooftop patio. He had a couple of bookcases that he used to store his possessions such as shoes, books, canning jars filled with coins, etc. I thought it was cute that a guy living alone had a candle on the table and some small ceramic animals you might find on grandma's shelf.

We tried to get the Popcorn Hour to work on Rhys's TV, but no luck. It was 8 p.m. when we sat down in the kitchen and put his computer on the table. We called our mutual friend Tony, who didn't want to connect with us in person because he had to work early the next morning. Using Skype, we had Tony join us at the kitchen table via Internet for a glass of wine. Rhys took two large water glasses from the cupboard and filled them with red wine. "Geez! You pour wine like you pour beer! That is a lot of wine!" I said. "Yeah, so?" replied Rhys. Then Tony held his glass of wine up to the computer screen and we toasted our little get-together.

We were having fun talking about dating, commitment, and what's wrong with men and women, etc. It felt like Tony was actually in the room. Then, a knock at the door brought in another friend of Rhys, and we were a party of four. This new addition was a bit of a character. Picture the tall, frizzy-haired eccentric Kramer from *Seinfeld* and you are on the right track. He appeared jittery and was smoking excessively. Rhys, Tony, and I were content with wine, but the K-Man look-alike wanted weed. He pulled a joint out of his pocket and lit up. We sat around talking together for the rest of the evening, and I enjoyed being a part of this new culture. The guys really wanted to know what women expect from a man during the courting period. Do women think a guy is considerate if he delays in seeking the first kiss? Or do they think he lacks confidence and a sense of romance? They were curious why women suffered such insecurity about their bodies. Men seem to be more comfortable naked than women do. Unfortunately, I didn't have any concrete answers. Every woman is different, but I did say that in most cases a woman's body language offers clues.

At one-thirty in the morning, I walked outside to go home, and during the six hours I had been at Rhys's place, a ton of snow had fallen. This was the most snow I had seen so far in Graz. It was magical! There were no car tracks or footprints -- nothing but beautiful, untouched snow. There was a full moon shining down on the snow-covered trees, and it still was snowing hard. During the tram ride home, I could swear I heard sleigh bells! I had gone skiing on many snowy mountains, but this was different. As I walked through the courtyard of my building, I really felt the transformation winter had made in the landscape, and the feeling it gave me was not one of barrenness but rather of mystery, even wonder. The full moon gave the snow a blue-colored shimmer, and everything sparkled. I tried to capture it on film, but I couldn't do it justice. Well, it's hard to sum up the effects of winter's sights on our perceptions and spirits: how can you really capture the complexity of the whole affair?

RABBIT HOLE

Winter weather continued through March, and I hadn't been working on obtaining a visa as I had planned. I was getting frustrated with the fact that the requirements were constantly changing. When traveling, I would just cross my fingers each time I went through passport control. My passport was created before microchips were required. I traveled enough to where I had country stamps on top of country stamps. Even I could not decipher how long I had been in the European Union. My passport was going to expire soon, and my next one would contain the microchip that would make my travel data readily available, making it impossible for me to remain in Europe illegally. On my most recent trip, I had a couple glasses of wine during the flight so I could get some sleep. When I was questioned by passport control about the number of days I had been in the E.U., I fumbled for answers. I was nervous about getting through so I came across as very awkward. Then, the officer asked me if I had been drinking. I responded with, "Absolutely! That was a thirteen-hour flight!" He laughed and waved me through.

Back in Graz, I was spending more time with a new friend Charity. Charity had contacted me through the InterNations website, looking for

English-speaking friends. She had moved to Graz with her Austrian fiancé, Gunter, and her two daughters aged four and twelve. We scheduled to meet at the fountain in Hauptplatz and then go to lunch. When our eyes met for the first time we were instantly friends. She had a great smile and a sunny disposition. It's funny how having the same language in common can be all you need to feel a connection with someone in a foreign country. At lunch Charity told me her story. She was divorced, living in Texas and meeting people on Internet dating sites when she met Gunter. Gunter, aged thirty-eight, was a few years older than Charity and from Austria. He was in Texas for business reasons and had free time to meet new people. She said that her friends were skeptical about Gunter because he told many stories about foreign travels and secret government meetings. According to Gunter, he was a foreign diplomat with the Austrian Embassy, but he had no clear story of why he was in Texas. Charity didn't care what anyone else thought. She was smitten with this charming Austrian man and his engaging accent. After a short courtship Gunter proposed, and wanted Charity and her daughters to move to Graz where they would set up house and obtain the necessary visas. When I met Charity, she had been in Graz for approximately five months. Over the next few weeks, Charity and I would occasionally meet for lunch or drinks in the evening where we would talk about the events of the day. Mostly, Charity complained about the difficulties she was facing with her daughters getting into the Austrian school system.

One evening, Charity invited me to join her and a new friend of hers for dinner. We went to meet Sarah at her apartment, bottle of wine in tow. Sarah was a twenty-something opera singer in Graz. She was tall and thin, and had long brown hair. We sat at her dining-room table in a tiny kitchen that reminded me of college housing apartments in the States. What we all had in common was our desire to make it in Austria. Sarah was originally from the US. She had performed in a few different countries in Europe before settling in with an opera company in Graz. That evening in her apartment, she invited us to attend one of her upcoming performances. The company she worked with was scheduled to perform Verdi's *La Traviata*.

I invited my friend Rhys to join us, and on opera night Gunter, Charity, Rhys and I got all dressed up and went together to the beautiful opera house. It was amazing. The ornate ceilings and chandeliers were breathtaking. This was the most beautiful venue I had ever visited. The evening started with glasses of champagne and our meandering through the crowds of exquisitely dressed patrons. Being seated in the red-velvet-draped opera hall as the symphony commenced was magical. It was delightful to watch knowing that I actually knew one of the singers! Sarah's performance was perfect, and we all applauded her when she met us outside. The five of us spent the rest of the evening at the nearest pub celebrating.

The next day, Charity called and said that Gunter wanted to talk to me. She said that he insisted we talk in person and that I should bring my passport. They both knew about my ongoing battle to obtain a visa, and perhaps he had a solution. I met her at the tram stop and we walked to her place.

Charity's apartment in Graz was very large, with extremely high ceilings, huge rooms, and wood floors. It looked more like a mansion than an apartment. Charity's two daughters played in their bedrooms while she searched for Gunter. When he appeared from a dark corridor, we adjourned to the kitchen table sitting across from one another. He asked if I had brought my passport, and I showed him that and all of my visa paperwork. He said that he didn't need anything except my passport information. He told me that he knew someone who would hire me on paper, and I could get a work visa allowing me to stay in Europe for three to five years. I wouldn't actually work for anyone.

He explained that I would receive a special card to use at passport checkpoints and another card that covered all of my health insurance. While he was talking he pulled out his phone and I saw the screen light up with bold letters: INTERPOL. He entered my first and last name and my passport number. Then, the screen flashed: NUMBER OF OFFENSES - 0. "Perfect!" Gunter exclaimed. "You are clean!"

Gunter told me that the employer would take care of all the paperwork and my nonexistent paychecks. All I had to do was pay the 140 euro a month for the insurance that the company was required to provide. I needed health insurance, so that sounded good to me. He said that we needed to get everything pushed through quickly, before the new work visa requirements were put into place the following month. I believed that to be true, because they were always adding new requirements and you never knew what they were going to be.

Gunter said that within the next ten days, we would go to Vienna together to finalize everything, and there we would meet my new "employer."

"His name is Martin," Gunter said with his heavy Austrian accent. "He will be nervous, because we could all be in a lot of trouble for this. I reassured him that he could trust you because I am sleeping with you." I thought to myself, "What? Why would he have to say that he was sleeping with me?"

He said that Martin's company shipped supplies, arms, and government controlled packages to Switzerland, Russia, and the U.S. "Wait, did you say arms? Would I be 'working' for an arms dealer?" I asked. "No," Gunter answered. "These are government-sanctioned contracts, all legal. We will leave in a few minutes to go to your bank for eight hundred euro to pay six months in advance for the insurance, and then to a photo shop to get three passport photos taken. We will then go to an office to print out the application forms in German, and I will also need a copy of your education diploma. What we are trying to accomplish here can't be discussed with anyone. You need to know that some of the people Martin works with are the type that if you cross them they will kill everyone in your house, including the goldfish."

At that moment, Gunter stepped outside to make a phone call, and Charity walked in with a bottle of wine in her hand and asked, "Would anyone like some cake?"

Staring down at my plate of cake, I felt lightheaded. This was all too crazy for me to process. Was this my chance to get a visa, or was this an elaborate scam? I trusted Charity, but Gunter was very abrupt and crass.

Gunter came back into the room, and we all finished our cake. "Okay, let's go!" Gunter ordered. I gave Charity a panicked look, and she smiled, saying, "Welcome to my new world! Every day I ask myself, what the hell am I doing?"

Between working on her kids' school enrollment, German classes, visa issues, and general navigation of the cities' bureaucracy, Charity was overwhelmed. You name it, and she had come up against a brick wall concerning it. She assured me, "It will be okay, Gunter always comes through in the end."

Gunter and I walked to the tram, and he lectured me the entire time. "You must get a man here to take care of you! This, what we are doing, will work, but if you want to live here permanently, you must get a man. You don't have to love him, but he can take care of you!" This was getting crazier by the minute.

We had my three passport photos taken and then a color copy of my passport. We went to the bank, and I withdrew the eight hundred euro and gave it to Gunter. Then we went to get the application forms. Gunter and I sat down at a nearby park to fill them out. I wrote everything down in German with his help. My head was spinning. I couldn't decide if I was being conned or if he was really trying to help me.

When we were finished, we returned to their apartment, where Charity was sitting in the living room with her kids. When Gunter left the room, Charity asked, "What happened? You look like you've seen a ghost!" I told her I wasn't sure about any of this and that I would talk to her later when I got home.

I then waited to hear further instructions from Gunter. There wasn't anything I could do but cross my fingers and hope that I hadn't made a colossal mistake. Had I made such a mistake?

WE LEAVE AT MIDNIGHT

In the weeks that followed, I didn't see much of Gunter. Charity had mentioned that he traveled a lot, but I should be hearing about my visa status as soon as he returned. Charity and I would meet with her youngest daughter for walks in the park a few times a week. She soon began sharing more details about her relationship. She said that Gunter had been alienating her from her friends and family. When she wanted to spend time talking to her parents on the phone, Gunter would come up with an excuse for them to leave and run errands. When she wanted to have a night out with friends, he insisted that he should go along, too. He was trying to control her by isolating her.

One night, I invited Charity to join me for a glass of wine. She said that Gunter would not be happy with that, but I said that he could join us a little later, allowing us to talk without him. Grudgingly, Gunter agreed. When Charity arrived at the restaurant, she looked hopeless. She said that Gunter was having money problems and was taking it out on her and the kids. She said that everything was falling apart and Gunter wasn't the man she thought he was. With tear-filled eyes she said she wanted to go back home to Texas, but she knew Gunter would not allow that -- he would prevent that from happening. One night he came home and they had a fight during which he hit her. Charity still believed he had some authority in Austria, but I didn't believe that anymore.

Two days after that conversation, Charity called me in a panic. "I can't take it anymore," she said. "Gunter came home and told me that we have to move to Slovakia. I just got my kids into school in Austria, and now he wants us to pack up and move to Slovakia! I know that if I tell him that I want to go back home to Texas, he will try to stop me. I already contacted my parents and they booked a flight for my kids and me. We need to be at the airport in Vienna by 6:00 a.m. tomorrow."

I was shocked. This was all happening so fast. Then she said, "Gunter will be out of the house tonight at 10:00, and I am going to leave after he's gone. I will take the train from Graz to Vienna. It only takes two-and-a-half hours to get there." I told her to hold on a minute while I made a call to my friend Tony, who was the train conductor in Graz. Tony said that the last train from Graz to Vienna left at 9:00 p.m. I then called my friend Rhys and asked him if he would be willing to give Charity and her kids a ride to Vienna. He said that the airport was closed for a few hours each night, so the best time to leave Graz would be at midnight. That way they would be open and we wouldn't have to wait in the car. He said that he would be happy to help.

I called Charity with the new plan, and all we needed now was a way for her to leave without Gunter knowing. She had her kids' things packed in their suitcases and threw some laundry over them so nothing looked suspicious. Now, all she had to do was wait for the right time to leave. At 5:00 p.m., I got the call. "Gunter just left to visit his mom for an hour. I have my friend Jehna waiting outside with her car. Can the kids and I stay with you at your place while we wait for Rhys?"

My mind was racing. "Yes, yes! You can hide out here." I remembered that when I filled out the supposed visa paperwork for Gunter, I gave him my address, but not my door number. I quickly went to each of my neighbors, asking them not to give anyone information about me just in case Gunter came looking.

I waited outside in front of my building, and just as Charity and the kids pulled up, my phone rang. It was Gunter. "Diane, Charity has left me!" I motioned to Charity not to get out of the car, and indicated that Gunter was on the phone. Gunter screamed frantically, "Did you hear me? Charity has left me!" I played dumb and said, "What are you talking about? She is probably out shopping or something." Gunter's voice intensified. "No! She is gone, really gone!" I asked him, "Did you guys have a fight?" "No! No fight! She just left! Did she say anything to you?"

I told him that I hadn't heard from her. I asked him how Charity would be able to leave with all of her belongings and children without any help, and he said he had no idea. I told him that maybe she just needed a little space and she would eventually come back. He calmed down and said, "You don't understand. She left a note in the kitchen saying that she is going back to Texas and will not be returning. She said that she didn't want to see me again." I did my best to sound surprised and ended the phone call, saying that I was sorry that she was gone.

Right after that, I hustled Charity, her two kids, seven pieces of luggage, and their friend Jehna into my apartment. I quickly closed the drapes, put on a Disney movie for the kids, and poured wine for the adults. By now it was 6:00 p.m. With the kids settled in with popcorn and blankets in the other room, Charity, Jehna, and I sat in disbelief of what was taking place. "You are fleeing the country at midnight!" I said.

My kitchen was small, so Jehna took a spot on the floor and asked if I had any vodka. "This is as good a time as any to have a stiff drink," proclaimed Charity. I put a bottle of vodka on the table, but a small glass of wine was fine for me. I was worried that Gunter would come blasting through the door and scare us all. I had to keep my wits about me.

I noticed Jehna was very supportive of Charity. She had been a friend for a few months and had gotten to know the family pretty well. I had an inkling that she didn't like Gunter from the start. Although Jehna was in her twenties she looked older. I got the impression that she had already had a hard life. She had dark hair and electric blue eyes that harbored sadness. She said that she had moved to Graz from Canada about a year previously to study law. "How impressive " I thought; to study law in a foreign language.

"I can't believe this is happening!" Charity said, with tears in her eyes. Jehna was encouraging and told Charity that she was doing the right thing. We ordered pizza and waited for Rhys. Time passed slowly, but promptly at midnight, Rhys showed up, and we loaded up the car. Jehna said her goodbyes to Charity and the kids while I joined Rhys in the car.

As if there wasn't enough drama already, we found ourselves driving through a rainstorm. The rain pounded down as we passed through road construction, closed off-ramp signs, and yellow caution lights. By the time we got to the airport, it was about 3:00 a.m. Most of the airport was closed, but we found an open check-in counter and a waiting area. Charity sobbed as we all hugged and said goodbye. The kids were exhausted, and we all just wanted the night to be over. Rhys was sweet and patient through the whole ordeal, and we didn't arrive back in Graz until seven-thirty in the morning. It was strange watching the sun come up from inside the car in our zombie-like state.

I went to bed and slept for about six hours when Gunter called. He said that he wanted me to come over and that he needed me as a friend. I told him that the only thing we had in common was the work visa he had promised me, and when he had more information on that, he could call me then. I never heard from him again.

Something good came from that outlandish night. Shortly after, Jehna became my best friend in Graz. Neither one of us felt the difference in our age mattered. We would spend hours together hiking, shopping, dining out and sharing our problems. We were each other's confidant and cheerleader.

ZOTTER

I kept my attendance up at the *Stammtisch* meetings. It was always nice to meet new people. At one of the gatherings the topic of discussion was the upcoming trip to the Zotter chocolate factory. Members from InterNations and *Stammtisch* had joined together to rent a large tour bus. This would be used for an hour-long trek through the Austrian countryside to the unique factory. It sounded like it would be a lot of fun, so I signed up. On the day of the tour, I took my seat near the front of the bus and started a conversation with the people closest to me. There was Vladimir and Dmitri from Russia, Rohit from India, and a few people from London and Korea. Outside the window, rolling hills and green farmland were pieced together like grandmother's quilt. Scattered about were many Austrian homes and churches.

Upon our arrival inside the factory, we were handed headsets with the choice of English or German recordings for the self-guided tour. My friend Rhys was with me, so we partnered up for the chocolate extravaganza. It started with tasting cocoa powder at various stages of preparations paired with the history of production on our headsets. Next we walked through a maze of windows with views of cocoa plants, large vats of chocolate and assembly lines of chocolate trays. At the bottom of a ladder-like staircase was a room with many containers of melted chocolate. We were provided ceramic spoons for sampling various liquid chocolates. The problem was that I wasn't aware of how extensive this tour was, and I should have paced myself. They all tasted so good, and I ate too much too soon. While walking through the factory, we found many different stations that served pieces of candy bars, melted chocolate, hot chocolate, and chocolate-covered nuts and berries. By the end, I could only manage to look, not taste. The tour ended at a little café where our group was able to sit and enjoy a savory dinner.

Seated at my table were some of my *Stammtisch* friends. We enjoyed group discussions, and on this particular evening, the conversation quickly turned to the differences between the ways we celebrate our winter holidays. Everyone had their own interesting story, but I found the Austrians' the most fascinating. Apparently, every year one night in December is spent with men dressed up like demons running through the streets terrorizing children! They do this to put everyone in mind of Krampus, a strange figure from Austria's regional folklore. Krampus is no Santa Claus -- instead, his job is to make children pay for their wicked behavior.

I can't imagine how terrifying this would be for the kids. My holidays were spent making my children feel happy and cherished. We looked forward to close family times together and stories of snowmen and reindeer. We might joke about how bad kids get coal in their stocking, but that is a far stretch from being beaten and kidnapped.

My fellow chocolate tasters said that in modern times the kids know that it is all in fun. It is toned down while the children are awake, and the craziness occurs after they are asleep. The adults turn the whole thing into a party.

It was past sunset on the bus ride home, and most of us slept through the trip in a sugar-induced coma.

MIXNITZ

It was a picturesque, sunny day when Rhys called and invited me to go with him and his mother to Bärenschützklamm Gorge near Mixnitz, Austria. This was an almost 1200 foot, near vertical climb up wooden bridges and ladders. I had heard about it, but had never been there. Rhys said that it was a great place to spend a warm afternoon hiking through beautiful mountains and waterfalls. They picked me up in Rhys's car at two in the afternoon, and after one hour of driving we were in the parking lot at the base of the mountain. We parked the car and grabbed a large bottle of drinking water from the back seat.

It took almost an hour to hike to the actual entrance of the attraction. We walked uphill the entire time on a dirt path that meandered through streams, rocks, and cliffs. The path was really rough, with tree roots and crevasses. I was glad we had brought the water. It was getting hot, and the steep walk was tiring.

After crossing over several wooden bridges, I could see why the trip was worth it. What an amazing place! There were large rock formations towering above, with countless aqua blue waterfalls everywhere. The rest of the journey was on bamboo-like ladders that were winding through tight cracks in the mountain and over pools of water that overflowed into one another. The grey stone walls of the mountain made the greens of the foliage and the blues of the water positively glow -- I have never seen anything quite like it. At times, the path was so steep that we used our hands and feet to climb up the ladders. We passed over, under, and behind waterfalls that were so beautiful it was hard to pay much-needed attention to safety.

It took at least four hours for us to make it to the top. On the last leg of our journey, I noticed that we kept passing people who were on their way down. There wasn't anyone else climbing up, but I was sure Rhys knew what he was doing.

At the top was an open field with a log-cabin-style restaurant. We ordered some hot dogs and sat outside at a picnic table. While enjoying my snack, I took in the glorious landscape and watched the shadows fall upon the forest. It was approximately 7 p.m., and we were the only people there. That added a certain solitude to the remarkable beauty of the place.

When I mentioned that it would be dark soon, Rhys said not to worry, because we would not be going down the same way we came up. There was a different path that didn't have any ladders, and it would lead us to the car. We got up and started our descent. We were surround by tall trees and walking on a narrow, rock-crammed dirt trail. Rhys stopped at a sign posted on the side of the trail that read, THREE-HOUR WALK TO PARKING LOT.

The sun had already begun to disappear behind the mountains. The three of us realized that in a matter of minutes we would be hiking in complete darkness. Undaunted, Rhys led the way while his mother trailed behind. We were going as fast as we could, but the ground was uneven and therefore very difficult to hurry through. It wasn't long before we couldn't see anything at all. A full moon would have been appreciated, but no such luck. The three of us were stumbling and falling, so we joined hands and took one tiny step at a time.

I was terrified. I could hear the water rushing by and knew that both sides of the trail had cliffs and waterfalls. There weren't any guardrails or protective barriers to prevent us from walking off a cliff to our death. There were mini paths that shot off from the main path; one wrong turn could have led us deeper into the forest and further from the parking lot. I suggested that we sit down and wait till morning. I just didn't think we could manage our way in pitch darkness. As I was pleading my case, Rhys's mother stopped mid-trek and said, "Oh my God, would you look at the stars! I have never seen so many stars!" Part of me admired her ability to take in the beauty of the night, but the rest of me thought, "Are you crazy? We are in jeopardy!"

I asked Rhys if he could use his cell phone as a flashlight, and he said, "Good idea!" We spent the next two hours intermittently lighting the way with his phone. Finally, we reached a paved road with dim streetlights. The danger was over, and we walked the rest of the way to the safety of our car.

More adventure than I had bargained for when agreeing to go on this hike. The first half was stunningly gorgeous, the second half petrifying.

FARGO AND THE TITANIC

Another winter had arrived in Graz when I realized that I had over-stayed my legal welcome according to visa regulations. I needed to leave Europe for a few weeks, so I booked a flight to the states to visit family and friends. My trip included a two-hour layover in Toronto, Canada. I found a spot near my gate to wait for my next flight. That was when I found myself looking out the airport windows at the "Storm of the Century." The snow was coming down hard with the wind blowing it sideways. Visibility was only a few feet and the tarmac was covered in snow. After an hour of nervously checking the flight monitors one by one, I found that every flight was listed as delayed or canceled. Then the dreaded announcement echoed over the loudspeakers: "all flights canceled." The look of fear that came over everyone's face and the panicked stampede that followed is something I will never forget.

I knew that hundreds of people had the same goal: grab your luggage and run for the door to get a hotel room. I had checked my luggage, and had to wait in a long line to retrieve it. I then stood in another line to get a hotel reservation, and luckily, I got one. Then, I ran past the longest files of people I had ever seen. There were people in one line trying to get hotel vouchers. There were people in another line trying to reschedule their flights, but the longest of all was the one to get a taxi out. There were a great many people crowded between the exit doors and me.

I remembered that there was a second floor that led to another taxi area, so I ran for it, but that line was even worse. I returned to the previous level and made my way through the crowd to the sidewalk. There I was informed that no taxis were running because of the snowstorm. The only transportation available was the hotel courtesy vans.

The snow coming down was relentless and the wind-chill made it even colder. I was dressed for a warm flight, not for standing on a frozen sidewalk in a storm. Compounding the problem was that there were only a few vans, and each one barely held eight people at a time. Each time a van pulled up to the sidewalk, people pushed their way through to surround it. It took over an hour for a van to return because the weather was so bad. I waited three long hours in the snow for my seat in one of those vans.

Everyone squeezed in, and it took forty-five minutes to drive very slowly to the hotel. I'm sure that with better weather it would have been a quick ten-minute trip. Inside, the hotel lobby was packed with people and again there were more lines to check in. I finally made it to my room and then down to the bar to get something to eat. Everyone was in the same boat, so we all had something in common.

The bar became the place to be. Everyone was telling their stories of how the storm had affected their travels. I talked to families, businessmen, and women of all ages, all stranded, but all thankful to be in a warm place.

The next morning I looked out my window and saw that the storm looked just as bad as the day before. I called the airlines, and they said that they had not yet canceled my flight, so I packed up and took the slow van back to the airport. I had to go through customs again and fill out the declarations form. I checked my luggage and waited in the lounge area. No flights had taken off yet, but they still listed my flight as on time. I had two hours left before my flight, so anything was possible. I watched out the window as the snow formed miniature tornados.

Thirty minutes before my scheduled departure, the loudspeaker came on in the terminal: "We regret to inform you that all flights have been canceled. We apologize for the inconvenience." I ran with the crowd of people to retrieve my luggage and head for the taxi herd. By the time I got there, it was even worse than the day before. People were sitting on the floor, trying to console their children. Fathers left their families inside while they braved the cold to find a hotel van. Inside, everyone pressed up against the windows to try to see if there was any progress. Outside, the mayhem repeated itself with everyone pushing to get a ride. Again, I waited about three hours before I got a seat in a van. I felt miserable as I looked out the window at the never-ending storm. Back at the hotel, it was the same as the night before, but with a little less enthusiasm.

The next morning, I repeated the routine from the day before. I called the airlines, verified that they hadn't canceled my flight, and headed to the airport. Again, the storm hadn't improved, but I had to try. I checked my luggage and went through customs. This time, I grabbed a few extra declarations forms, just in case. I might as well have them filled out in advance. I waited for two-and-a-half hours in the lounge when that familiar sound of the loudspeaker came on: "We regret to inform you that all flights have been canceled. We apologize for the inconvenience."

The events that had happened the day before were happening again, but people were getting tired. I saw more arguing and less patience. I saw pained faces and children crying. The elderly seemed to have given up completely. They just sat down on the floor with their luggage. No one wanted to wait outside in the storm. We all tried to watch for the hotel vans from inside and fight through to the outside when one pulled up. It was a little like *Fargo* meets *The Titanic*.

The third day was the same. The storm hadn't let up. Once the formalities and necessities were done, I waited in the airport lounge, looking out the window at the snow tornados. This time, when the loudspeaker announced that all the flights had been canceled, I felt a tear run down my face. Once again, I waited in all the lines and made it to the taxi mob.

I didn't think it was possible, but the situation was worse than the days before. I knew that if I didn't stand in the snow and fight for a spot, I might not get to the hotel at all. I waited for two hours in the freezing cold and then saw a van approaching. I pushed my way through to the driver's side, and with tears in my eyes, told him that I didn't think I could wait any longer. He opened up the passenger side door and told me to get in while he put my luggage in the back.

As he stepped away, a woman shoved me to the curb and took my seat. The driver returned and said that he was sorry, but there wasn't anything he could do about it. He removed my luggage from the van and handed it back to me. My feet were frozen, and I didn't have any gloves, so my hands were red and painful. I couldn't move very well because I had lost feeling in my legs. I could feel the cold concrete beneath my feet, and my face was numb. The tears just came and I gave up, shaking my head. The driver looked at me through the snow-filled air and yelled "I will send someone for you, I promise. When the next van comes, tell him this password: double-o-seven." Then he drove away, leaving my luggage and me behind.

An hour passed while I waited for the next van. I found it hard to keep my misery to myself. Without my consent, my mouth started humming and it sounded a little like whining. My teeth were chattering, and I still couldn't move my legs at all. My face froze in a pained position, and I looked pathetic. A kind gentleman introduced himself as Gus and offered me his coat. I couldn't accept and leave him coatless but I thanked him. We stood side by side shivering. When I caught a glimpse of an upcoming van, I bolted towards it, running alongside while it was still moving. I grabbed the door handle and the driver yelled "Wait for me to park!" "Double-o seven!" I screamed. To that, the driver yelled, "Oh! Get in!" As I jumped into the van I told the driver that he needed to let my partner Gus in as well. Everyone including Gus piled in and silently watched out the van windows as we slowly snowplowed our way back to the hotel.

I thought that would be my only breakdown, but there was one more to come. The next day -- the fourth -- it was the same routine, but when I reached the customs checkpoint, I lost it. I just stood there motionless; crying, saying I couldn't go any further. The very nice officers behind the desk said, "Come on! You can do this! Just do it one more time!" I wiped my tears and did it one more time. The flight took off that day. I had spent four days in Toronto, but I will always remember it as Fargo.

The history books rightly remind us how much progress we have all made since the days when you couldn't travel more than a few miles without risking life and limb. Even so, modern travel has ordeals all its own. This one that I went through reminded me of the sheer difficulty that comes with moving large numbers of people at the same time: simple delays, "logistics," had created a fiendishly particular kind of panic and misery for countless individuals who were just trying to make their way home, or wherever they needed to be.

MARIBOR, SLOVENIA

My visit with family and friends helped me to forget about the "Storm of the Century" and I enjoyed the creature comforts of home. My stay was a couple of weeks and then I headed back to Graz.

A few months later, I spent some down time perusing the InterNations website. I found quite a few interesting events coming up, but one in particular caught my eye. I saw an invitation to the fifty-fifth anniversary party for a museum in Maribor, Slovenia. I knew that Slovenia bordered Austria and wouldn't be too far away, so I pressed the "Accept Invitation" button without giving much thought to whether or not I'd actually go. Two days later, I received an email from another InterNations member who was attending the same event. She wrote that she was glad to see someone from California was coming, and that she, too, was from California. She left me her phone number and email address.

Her name was Yolanda, and I phoned her that afternoon. We talked for at least half an hour. Her father was from Slovenia, and her mother was from Guadalajara. They met in Pasadena, California, where they raised Yolanda and her siblings. Yolanda moved to Vienna, Austria, thirty years ago. She said that if I wanted, she and her husband Tony could pick me up in Graz on their way to Maribor. It turned out that the museum was honoring Yolanda's father, but he was too old to make the trip, so Yolanda was going to accept the award in his honor. I thought it would be great to go with someone associated with the event, so I booked a hotel for two nights. Four days later, I stood on the sidewalk in front of my flat with my suitcase in tow waiting for Yolanda and Tony to pick me up. It crossed my mind that it was a little crazy to yet again jump into a car with strangers headed to another country. But Yolanda sounded sweet, so this could be another entertaining adventure.

I knew in an instant that I liked them. Yolanda, who looked to be in her forties, was wearing a brightly colored sundress that showed off her pretty brown skin and dark black hair. She greeted me with a cheerful smile and a hug. She introduced me to her husband Tony, who was Austrian. Gray-haired and short of stature, he looked older than Yolanda. He spoke perfect English with an Austrian accent. He, too, was very jolly. I hopped in the back seat of their car and off we went. We talked nonstop all the way to Maribor, sharing our experiences of expat life.

When we arrived, I found Maribor to be quite charming. This was a very old city with architecture not so different from Austria, but it had a different feel. It was a lot smaller than Graz, and less affluent. Yolanda and Tony were kind enough to drop me off at my hotel. They gave me a hand-drawn map so I could find my way to the museum event, and we agreed to meet there. I checked into my room and went outside to take a peek at the surrounding area.

For such a small place, there was a lot to see. There was a large brass statue in the shape of an impressive abstract orb in the center of the city. There were little streets lined with trees, and I saw a colorful display of open umbrellas suspended overhead like a quilt above a courtyard. The vibrant colors of the umbrellas against the blue sky were breathtaking. I found a few fountains and parks, but every statue and landmark was inscribed in Slovenian, so I didn't know what I was seeing. Even so, I was happy to take it all in as an aesthetic experience rather than a learning one -- travel doesn't always need to be about amassing knowledge, after all. I took a walk along the Drava River and found a path to restaurants and some interesting shops and cafés.

It was almost time to find the museum, so after changing into something less casual, I set out -- with no expectations -- to the event. The setting was a grassy courtyard behind the museum. There were many chairs set up, all facing the beautiful entrance of the building. Long tables adorned with fruit platters, wine glasses, and candelabras were set up on the grass, with formally dressed waiters applying their finishing touches. All of the chairs were full, so I took my place leaning up against a pillar behind everyone.

The speeches that night were all in Slovenian. When the talking stopped, Yolanda took the stage, and they presented her with a large bouquet of flowers and a regal-looking medal in honor of her father. She then took her seat as a group of four festively dressed men sang beautiful songs. The reception after the ceremony was great. The local newspaper photographed Yolanda, Tony, and me, and everyone wanted to have a chance to congratulate Yolanda. After champagne and strawberries, it was time to tour the museum.

Inside, the mood was somber. The entire museum was full of photographs and memorabilia from World War II. The Nazis occupied Slovenia during that time and killed many Slovenians. Tony, who had relatives from Maribor, stood in front of a wall inscribed with the names of all the children who were put to death. I saw his eyes tear up, and I didn't know what to say, so I just placed my hand on his shoulder to express my feelings. As we walked the museum together, Yolanda told me the story of her own father's escape from Slovenia.

When the Nazis took over, Yolanda's father was a soldier. Not wanting to be part of the German occupation, he fled to his mother's home. His plan was to fight his way through the necessary European borders and eventually make his way to the United States. Before he was able to leave, they got word that the troops were on their way to stop him. His mother had a hole in her backyard that he could fit in. She buried him in the ground with a small hose to breathe out of. After a thorough search, the Nazis gave up and left. He had to say goodbye to his mother. It was extremely difficult, but he was able to make it all the way to California, where, at age ninety-four, he currently lives.

We spent about an hour touring the museum and then the three of us went to dinner together. We found a delightful restaurant where we sat outside at a candlelit table. We talked and laughed for at least two hours, enjoying great food and wine. My hotel was around the corner, so when we ended our evening, I walked back to my room.

The next morning, I walked around Maribor and looked inside all of the cute shops that lined the streets. After enjoying a nice lunch outside I decided I had seen enough and thought I might as well go home that day. Yolanda and Tony were staying for the week, so I booked a train back to Graz. I didn't have any plans for that evening, so I went back to the hotel and told the front desk I was checking out one day early. The kind woman working the desk said it wasn't a problem, and I went upstairs to pack.

Down in the lobby, while waiting for a taxi, I got a phone call from Yolanda. "Join us for dinner tonight!" I looked down at my suitcase and thought, "Why not?" The woman at the front desk checked me back into the same room. I unpacked, put on a nice dress and headed out.

Yolanda and Tony were staying at a ski lodge nestled in the nearby mountains. They invited me to join them for dinner at the lodge, where large chandeliers hung above the spacious dining room. After dinner, we went to the hotel bar where a DJ was playing old Frank Sinatra songs. We had so much fun laughing and singing together. At the end of the night, they walked me to my taxi, and we all hugged goodbye.

The next morning, I boarded the train to Graz, where I stared dreamily out the window, thinking about how great Yolanda and Tony were, and how happy I was to be a part of their trip. In spite of my solitary jaunt, thanks to my fellow travelers I ended up learning a great deal about Slovenia and its harrowing World War II experience.

DARK

After spending a month in the US visiting friends and family, I came back to Graz. I knew my flat would be freezing in March, and it usually took a couple of days to warm up enough for me to get out of bed. I arranged for a hotel room nearby for the first night. After turning up the heat at my place, I checked in to the hotel. I called my friend Jehna to join me for dinner and drinks. It was great! We had a glass of wine in the room and then went to a nice Italian restaurant, where we dined on too much pasta and more wine.

Getting back to the hotel, we saw that the hotel bar was still open. There were a few people there, and we sat down at a small table near the lobby. The bartender was very friendly and offered us shots of tequila on the house. I usually don't drink tequila, but he made it sound so festive that I could hardly refuse. A few minutes passed, and he brought by another round. I insisted that it be the last and that he should charge it to my room. Jehna and I said good night, and she headed home. I signed the bar bill and went up to bed. I was fast asleep when I heard knocking at my door. I could hear the bartender's voice on the other side calling my name.

What the hell? I decided to stay quiet, and thought that if I did maybe he would go away. I went back to sleep, but about an hour later, I woke up with the bartender on top of me, raping me. He had waited till the bar was closed and used a manager's key to let himself into my room. This was all too horrible and confusing. I quickly shoved him to the floor and started yelling at him to get out. My memory of that evening is foggy, but here is what I remember. I picked up the hotel phone and called Jehna. It was approximately 3 a.m. I told her that I had been raped and that I needed her to call the police for me. In the states I would have called 911, but I didn't know what number to call in Austria. Jehna was shocked to hear what had happened, and she called the police for me and said that she and her boy-friend would meet me at the hotel.

Getting exceedingly upset, I rushed downstairs and demanded to see the manager. The young man behind the counter looked at me, and based on the guilty look on his face I believe he knew what had happened. He yelled for Scott the bartender to come over. I panicked and screamed "No! Not Scott!" I ran past the desk and down the nearest flight of stairs to the restrooms. I hid behind a locked stall door. Scott quickly appeared and from the other side of the door he pleaded with me. "There is no need for a manager, don't tell anyone anything." I let him know that the police had already been called and were on their way. My next memory is of me sitting in the hotel lobby with Jehna, her boyfriend, Scott, the hotel manager, and the police. The police questioned everyone and then took all of us to the police station. I met with the detective assigned to my case where we filled out the formal charges against Scott, and then they drove me to a medical center for a proper rape kit process.

I must have blocked most of the rape from my memory because when I went to the bathroom the next day I saw that my legs were badly bruised. To this day I don't remember the violence that happened that night but I am thankful for that.

I had decided to go back to the US, so my case was expedited. I met with the attorney assigned to me and spent four hours in court giving my testimony, which was video recorded for future use.

After a couple of months passed, I decided to write a poem about that night to help me process what had happened. It is still distressing to talk about, so rather than try to do that in narrative form, at this point I will simply offer the poem itself:

DARK

The sun was shining, the people were friendly, music filled the air
Who knew what was in store for her
Who knew what one man would dare
She laughed with friends and enjoyed her night,
all the world was sparkling
Everything was perfect then
Unaware of dark clouds lurking
Then midst a summer's good night dream, the silence suddenly shattered
"What is this darkness that entered the room?"
"Why is everything so tattered?"
The room grew large, the ceiling pulled away, she suddenly felt so small
The walls caught fire, the candles went out
There was no one she could call
She fought alone till the nightmare ended,
or at least that's how it seemed
What lay ahead was so much worse
Her world forever changed, her inner light no longer beamed
Days have passed and life goes on, not quite sure how to process
Everything is different now
All that's left is time to heal this

Fast-forward one year and Scott was found guilty. Facing five years in prison, Scott filed an appeal. That took another year, and before the final verdict was rendered, Scott killed himself.

Tragic from beginning to end.

HIKE UP . . .
AMBULANCE DOWN

It was summer again when Christina had a few weeks off from vet school and came from Ireland to visit me in Graz. For some fun and exercise we planned a day trip to Mixnitz. Together with my friend Jehna, we took a quick train ride to the base of the mountain. This is the same place I had been to before with Rhys and his mother. The hike up takes about three hours. The contrast of gray rocks against turquoise water is breath taking. We took a two-minute break here and there, but mostly just kept on hiking.

It wasn't until we got to the grassy field at the top of the mountain that Christina told me she was experiencing a pounding heart rate. Her heart was racing, and she was feeling faint. She lay down on a bench attached to a picnic table to try to slow down her heart. We waited half an hour, but she showed no signs of improvement.

There was nothing we could do to help her. We had no choice but to head back down the mountain. I was extremely concerned because every five minutes Christina had to stop, sit down, and put her head between her knees. She was experiencing vertigo, and at one point she vomited. She looked up at me with tears in her eyes and said that she couldn't go any farther. She wanted Jehna and me to try to find someone to give her a ride down. Knowing that I didn't have the necessary skills to help her, I fought back tears. We were in the middle of a forest on a path that was hard on foot and impossible for any vehicle. We walked a little farther, and the path improved slightly. Christina lay down in the dirt in the fetal position. Meanwhile, Jehna and I rushed a few paces ahead and saw a farm in the distance with nine men seated at a table beneath a tree with a truck parked nearby. We ran towards the men and asked if anyone would be willing to give us a ride down the mountain. They didn't speak any English, so Jehna spoke to them in German. They were very reluctant. I didn't understand why they didn't see the urgency, but Jehna thought they didn't think we were in trouble, just that we were tired and wanted an easy way down. Jehna eventually convinced them that we were in serious trouble and that my daughter was too sick to continue. Finally, they all got up and followed us to where we had left Christina.

When we found her, she was still down in the dirt, crying. The owner of the truck drove over and helped Christina into the passenger side. I could tell that the men felt sorry for her, but there was only room for one passenger, so the remaining eight men, Jehna, and I hiked down to the halfway point. I wanted the driver to take her all the way down, but he said that he had already called for an ambulance. I ran and stumbled through the forest praying that when we made it to Christina she would be okay. It took us twenty-five minutes to reach her. I was beside myself with worry, afraid that Christina might not survive.

When the ambulance came up, they drove on a private government road that was accessed only by using a special key. They let Jehna and me join Christina in the ambulance, where they quickly put her on oxygen and drove us down the mountain. The color slowly came back to Christina's cheeks, and she said that she was starting to feel better. We phoned ahead to Jehna's boyfriend, who met us at the bottom of the mountain to give us a ride home.

I wanted Christina to go to the hospital, but she insisted that she was going to be fine and would see her own doctor back in Ireland. The total cost of the ambulance was twenty euros; I can imagine how expensive that would have been in the States -- several hundred dollars at the least.

Flash forward five months, and Christina was diagnosed with arrhythmia. She went into a hospital in Ireland, was treated, and is doing great.

AHOY!

After a few months alone in Graz, I wanted to visit Christina in Ireland. She only had one weekend available, so I thought a quick trip would be better than nothing. I booked a flight to Kinsale where Christina was staying with her boyfriend, Niall. Niall's place in Kinsale used to be a bed-and-breakfast inn. It sat along the seaside boardwalk of the most charming little community, small boats bobbing in the harbor surrounded by rolling green countryside. It was no longer used as an Inn, and Niall had the entire place to himself. Inside were seven bedrooms with the room numbers still on the doors. There was a central kitchen and a quaint living room. While Niall was at work, Christina and I spent the day shopping and catching up on each other's lives.

When Niall came home, the three of us went to dinner at a cool local restaurant. During our lovely meal, Niall talked passionately about a tall sailing ship that had recently sunk off the coast of Ireland near Kinsale. He talked about the interesting history behind that ship named the Astrid. Built in the Netherlands in 1918 as a cargo ship, the Astrid was transferred to Swedish ownership and worked the Baltic Sea trade routes until 1975.

After another sale, the ship was taken by Lebanese drug-smugglers. She was found abandoned and burnt to a shell off the coast of England in the early 1980s. A salvage operation saved her, and she was transformed into a training vessel for the Dutch. After her recent shipwreck the Astrid had been raised and dry-docked down the street from Niall's place.

Niall expressed his sadness when he learned that the ship was to be scrapped. As a nautical engineer, he wished he could save her, but it would take an enormous amount of money.

We finished our dinner and walked back to Niall's place. There, we poured three glasses of wine and took them with us on our walk to look at Astrid. It was after 10 p.m., so it was dark as we walked the quiet streets of Kinsale, lit by the golden light of the streetlamps. I mentioned to Niall that I thought it was great that we were allowed to walk around with a full glass of wine, and he responded with, "Oh no, this isn't legal. The cops are just asleep by now!"

A few more minutes' walk, and there she was. Looking so enormous, and raised high above the water, the black sky behind her. We hid our empty wine glasses near the fence surrounding the ship area, took a quick look around to see that no one was watching, and jumped the fence. I was amazed to see how far away the dry-docked ship was from the concrete platform we were standing on.

I told Niall that if the ship was going to be scrapped, he might as well take a souvenir. He paced back and forth, trying to find a way down to the metal barge beneath her. There was a rope ladder that hung down the wall near where we were standing, but Niall would have to jump from the bottom of the ladder to the barge. The distance between was about a four-foot expanse of water.

He decided it was worth a try, and down he went. Christina and I stood by, nervously watching as Niall landed on the barge and looked up at the thirty-foot-high deck of the ship. We talked back and forth in a whispered yell so we could hear each other, but not alert the village to the upcoming pillaging.

Niall was frustrated to learn that there wasn't any way up to the deck. All that was available were the long ropes used to tether the ship. He grabbed the closest one and tried to shimmy up the rope. Christina and I were pensive and silent as we watched him make it halfway up the rope, only to drop back down to the barge. He gave it another try, but again dropped back down. We saw that a different rope had a knot in it near the top that would help him get a better grip. He only had so many tries left in him before he would be too weak to make it, so it was now or never. He shimmied up the rope like a pirate, threw his body over the ship's railing, and stood on the deck! "Yeah!" Christina and I whispered loudly.

Niall used his cell phone to light his way through cabins. It was eerie to see the dim light travel from porthole to porthole. After a few seconds of banging noise, he emerged on the deck, holding something. He instructed Christina and me to lay his jacket on the platform where we were standing and then stand back. We took a few steps to the side and he threw down his finding, which landed squarely on his jacket.

It was a block. A block is a pulley used for controlling the angle of attack of the mainsail. Glorious! Niall disappeared into the cabin again and brought out another block and threw it successfully to our side. I was caught up in the excitement, and asked if he could find something for me. I said that a doorknob or hinge would be cool and Niall disappeared again. He came back with an old skeleton key. Perfect!

When Niall carefully made it back to us, we were intrigued by our stolen treasures. Just in case anyone heard the racket coming from the ship, we quickly grabbed our empty wine glasses and pirates' booty and headed towards Niall's place. We were five minutes into our walk when we saw a young couple walking towards us.

At the same time, a police car approached. The officers parked their car and walked in our direction. The three of us held our wine glasses and stolen goods, but for some reason, the cops wanted to talk with the young couple. We just kept walking, never looking back. We just had broken at least three laws, including trespassing, so I couldn't help but wonder what the young couple had done to get the attention of the police.

Back at Niall's, we celebrated with a bottle of French wine that was being saved for a special occasion. "This is a worthy occasion!" exclaimed Niall. We spent the rest of the night listening to Niall playing his guitar while we all sang.

What a magical night! A Disney-like setting lit by a full moon with a pirate adventure to boot. For some reason I found adventure more readily available in Europe than in the U.S. Perhaps when I'm in a foreign country I have a different mindset that lends itself to the unexpected. A favorite quote of mine is "Chance favors the prepared mind" by Louis Pasteur. For myself, this has proven to be true.

WHAT A JOURNEY

I moved to Graz to start a new life, learn a new language, meet new people, and learn about myself and the world around me. My goal was to grow as a person and become more enlightened. My experience was and still is so much more than I ever hoped.

The most impressive sight, I must say, was the ever-changing landscape -- from the dirt and concrete streets of Istanbul, with its tributes to textiles and spires, to the quaint streets and green-covered shorelines of Ireland. I enjoyed the never-ending roads that tunneled through the mountains of Croatia, and the golden glow of the city lights in Budapest and Spain. These things will enchant my imagination for the rest of my days.

Still, what I found most remarkable were the many deep conversations I was privileged to be a part of: talking about politics with Austrians, compassion with Russians, adventure with Slovenians, and history with every culture I encountered. All of the people I talked to knew their history; not just recent history, but also every battle and every event that affected their homeland and changed their surroundings. Their history is remembered in part because they keep it alive in daily conversation: for better or for worse, it's alive in the hearts and on the tongues of the people of Europe.

How different that is from so many of us here in the United States -- we seem to live mostly in the present, and we don't dwell much on the past.

I was fortunate to have these experiences, and I think the reason so many incredible things happened to me is that I showed up with my heart and mind wide open. I had no preconceived notions of foreign lands. I had no idea what I was doing, but I was ready for anything that came along. Quite simply, I was open to experience, and experience is what I got. Sometimes people ask me if I was ever afraid. No, I was never afraid, only excited to see what would happen next. Every day I walked out the door, not knowing what the day would bring. I was never disappointed. I am grateful for my European adventure, and I know that it has changed me for the better. Life is short, and when I approach the end of mine, I will be able to say with honesty that I lived, that I didn't let all my dreams pass idly by.